Advance Praise for
Outside Voices

"*Outside Voices* is a mesmerizing, lyrical account of the heady days of the women's movement in Berkeley in the 1970s. It's a blast to follow Joan Gelfand, newly arrived from New York and still reeling from the untimely death of her father, as she visits communes, cooks vegetarian food, listens to musicians in coffee shops, and poses nude for a painter who seduces her— just one of many wild experiences during the days of sex, drugs, and rock and roll. The heart of the book, however, is Gelfand's search for her poet's voice, something she discovers through the embrace of the women's community around her."

—**Frances Dinkelspiel**, cofounder of Berkeleyside and Cityside and author of
New York Times bestseller *Tangled Vines: Greed, Murder, Obsession
and an Arsonist in the Vineyards of California*

"Grieving the death of her father, trying to find herself as a poet, Gelfand takes the reader on a nostalgic through-the-looking-glass tour of the radical people and wild places in Berkeley that informed her career as a critic, teacher, and writer. '[I]n Berkeley,' the poet enthuses, 'spring is stretched out like a delicious piece of saltwater taffy, all sweetness and joy.'"

—**Barbara Quick**, novelist, poet, journalist, and author of *What Disappears*
and *Vivaldi's Virgins: A Novel*

"Berkeley in the 1970s was the bullseye of a cultural revolution that changed this country so profoundly that those who didn't live through it can hardly imagine what things were like before it happened. No one has captured this better than Joan Gelfand who in 1972 got on a plane in New York on a cold, leafless, grim Election day and six hours later stepped off of it into a sunny California afternoon where roses were blooming and where, when you knocked on the door, Opportunity answered, and you could find people who would help you live you the life you had always wanted to live.

"In Berkeley, Gelfand discovers a town that has a history of nurturing artists; a town where Second Wave Feminism is blasting open opportunities for women; a town where rents are low and she can eat "farm-to-fork" before the term was invented. As she finds her way as a poet, she takes us along into the communes, the newly created women-only spaces, and the gay bars where feminists are part of a new emboldened culture of resistance that includes not only the Black Panthers and the Anti-War Movement, but musicians, artists, alchemists, fruitarians, pescatarians, vegans, spiritual seekers, philosophers, dreamers, yogis, naturopaths, Buddhists, and union organizers.

"Gelfand's memoir is a wonderfully wild ride into a world so open, so creative, so ecstatic that it makes Paris in the '20s look like Indianapolis in the '50s. Fasten your seatbelts. This is a brilliant book, and if you want to know what the '70s were really like without dropping Acid and signing up for time travel, this is your ticket."

—**Mary Mackey**, *New York Times* bestselling author of fourteen novels and eight collections of poetry

OUTSIDE VOICES

A MEMOIR OF THE BERKELEY REVOLUTION

JOAN GELFAND

POST HILL
PRESS

A POST HILL PRESS BOOK

Outside Voices:
A Memoir of the Berkeley Revolution
© 2024 by Joan Gelfand
All Rights Reserved

ISBN: 979-8-88845-004-8
ISBN (eBook): 979-8-88845-005-5

Cover design by Conroy Accord
Interior design and composition by Greg Johnson, Textbook Perfect

This is a work of nonfiction. All people, locations, events, and situations are portrayed to the best of the author's memory.

Post Hill Press
New York ✦ Nashville
posthillpress.com

Published in the United States of America
1 2 3 4 5 6 7 8 9 10

For the children of my children—
Caleb, Mason, Theo, and Talia:
may you find your paths through the forest of life.

Contents

Boys vs. Girls (1965)

The morning breaks hot that Tuesday in late July. The sun bears down hard from its apex above the baseball diamond: high noon. Beneath the raucous shouts of prepubescent boys and girls rooting unabashedly for their teammates, the distinct sounds of bumblebees buzzing in the grass; cicadas' clacking and crickets' high-pitched hum provide ambient music.

We are in a grassy meadow in Woodridge, a small town deep in the heart of the Catskill Mountains. Far from the density and humidity of New York City's too-close streets and dirty alleys, baking brownstones and overheated concrete sidewalks, glass and steel high-rise apartment buildings. The town is our retreat from everything urban. Our skin has tanned to brown; our bodies grown fit from weeks of playing hard, kicking up dust, and swimming relay races in the large pool at the top of the hill. Surrounded by open green fields and blue skies, instead of the brick schoolyards of the inner cities where we live all year. Nature's sweet silence offers a respite.

We arrive en masse as soon as school lets out. Having made the lengthy drive up the concrete ribbon of road that is the New York

State Thruway, our families set up house in rustic bungalows. The colony's population hails from one end of greater New York City to another: Flatbush to Riverside, Flushing Meadows to Bayside, the Bronx to Westchester and the small suburban towns of Long Island. We drive in the white Impala from Forest Hills, a small community in Queens. Our commonality is a Jewish family: stay-at-home mom and a father who believes children need wide-open spaces and nature. Parents who agree that childhood is not complete without getting lost in the woods or picking buckets of ripe blueberries. This summer means discovering a pure water spring, its mellifluous fountain falling from deep within a rock cave, the water so sweet my mom cries, "Heaven!"

Ringing the field where the annual "Boys Against Girls" softball game kicks off are the white bungalows where our mothers listen to swing jazz on the radio and prepare lunch. The wooden structures are small compared to our city apartments but large enough for the little time we spend indoors. In the bungalows, a high riser doubles as a couch and extra bed; the wallpaper's faded roses and aging linoleum floor are acceptable décor to mothers who wouldn't deign to live without wall-to-wall carpet and curtains coordinated to match the bedspreads. There are no televisions, no telephones. The bungalows are like a cheerful daisy chain, a pastel-colored necklace of nuclear family nests. The grass is a deep emerald green from a recent summer rain.

Bases are loaded and the score is tied when I get up to the plate. We're holding our own, and Linda, my counselor, is screaming maniacally. I am two months from my twelfth birthday.

As we play, Linda, my counselor, cheers, "Come on, girls. You can do it! We're better than these boys any day!" Her encouragement is essential as we face off with boys whose pitching arms have been perfected with their dads for years.

2

Boys vs. Girls (1965)

Linda is like an older sister to us. Occasionally, on a quiet, sunny afternoon—tired of threading lanyards, throwing clay for clunky pottery, weaving potholders, and punching volleyballs—she lets us take a break from scheduled activities. Under the trees, we lie flat on our backs; girl bodies, scattered in the grass pointing out elephants and dinosaurs in the puffy white cumulous clouds. What could be more important on a summer afternoon than staring at clouds, talking about boys?

"How long have you been going steady with Scotty?" Leslie asks, wondering what it's like to have a real boyfriend, not just a boyfriend who steals kisses in the dark when we play spin the bottle. Not just a boyfriend you sneak glances at with your girlfriends, only to giggle when he catches you staring, but a real boy to talk to, go to the movies with, hold hands with in the ice cream shoppe.

"Two years," Linda answers.

"Wow! Are you going to marry him?" Ellen asks, sitting up now.

"Maybe."

We all hope so. Scotty and Linda look very nice together, especially since Linda got a nose job. They both are tall and thin, with dark hair. Linda seems to be always smiling; she and Scotty walk through the bungalow colony with their arms around each other's waists.

With Linda, we practice standing up straight. Laurie's grandmother has told her that she is round-shouldered so we join her in practicing standing erect. Don't get me wrong: we are not from the class of girls sent to finishing schools, but we know what it means to be a woman: be pretty and pleasant. Jewish women had bought into the American beauty standard. *Woman's Day, Redbook, Ladies' Home Journal* all made their way to mailboxes across the city and to kitchen tables. Hair bleaching, perennial dieting, and often (as in Linda's case) going under the knife with the goal of assimilating into the White Anglo-Saxon Protestant (WASP) culture. It is a symbol of pride and affluence. The *shtetls* are behind us: teeth straightened, nails manicured, frizzy hair tamed, pushed into rollers, and accosted with hot irons. The lithe blonde is our beauty model—although for most of us here, descended from peasant stock, the thin gene never made its way into our DNA. Still, we want the boys to like us the way Scotty likes Linda.

Linda is the oldest daughter of my parents' best friends, the Litwaks. Daddy and Sol Litwak are the "big men" of the bungalow colony: successful, ambitious, and tall, with generous personalities and gorgeous, small-boned wives with Marilyn Monroe dyed-blonde hair. The moms' concerns are confined to the four walls of their apartments and suburban homes: children, husbands, and the life challenges and choices of their friends and neighbors.

"Do you hear Jeannette is pregnant again?" Irma to my mom over mid-morning coffee.

"With her third?" my mother lit up another L&M.

"Yup. One more. I think she's worried Sol might be looking around, or at least that was the sense I got. A baby would bring his attention home."

"Oh, these men," my mother puffed her smoke up toward the ceiling. "Big talkers. They love the ladies but no way do they step out." I was stationed in the hallway, my secret spot when Mom had Irma and other girlfriends over. Only four, and not ready for school yet, I was more interested in hearing about Jeannette's pregnancy, Sheila's divorce, and Pansy's miscarriage than fantasy play with Barbies. There were only so many outfits I could change and scenarios I could make believe. Irma and my mom gossiped away, but when my mother wanted serious talk, she and Irma switched to Yiddish.

Daddy renovates warehouses in Soho in New York City from his office on Wall Street. Sol owns a car dealership, the lot filled with the dream cars of the '60s: Cadillacs, Bonnevilles, and Cutlass Supremes.

Boys vs. Girls (1965)

When I visited Daddy in his office, I saw his pencils chewed up and heard him yelling on the phone. When he hung up, we'd hit the toy store and the deli for comics and knishes and none of it matters for an hour.

Laurie is first at bat. Base hit. That girl just got up there, all business, with her small frame, tanned legs, pretty eyes, and dark hair pulled back in a ponytail. The bat connects with Alan's first pitch and she pounces, slamming one down the middle, missing the pitcher's glove. Billy, the pitcher, catches the ball mid-field while Laurie tags the dusty first base bag. She hovers, edging off the base to steal second.

The boys' coach, Richard, is getting nervous, telling his guys to stay on their bases. Laurie doesn't look round-shouldered to me. She looks proud!

Next up is Cora, our big girl. Cora can't run fast because of her weight but has a swing like Babe Ruth. This summer, her game has advanced to new heights. Her at-bats have become dependable base hits. And you'd better pay attention when Cora bats or you'd be at risk for losing an eye. Cora grabs the heaviest bat and whaps it between first and second. Two yards to the right and it would have been foul. Scott and Wayne scramble for the ball as Laurie runs to second and Cora makes it on to first.

Leslie, our gangly, long-legged girl with the squeaky voice and too-large nose is up next. Sensing a possible win, Linda becomes apoplectic. "Slam it, Les! Right down the middle!"

My hopes dwindle. Leslie's at-bats are infamously poor.

"We're dead," I whisper to Ellen, my best friend, whom the boys nickname "Jane Mansfield" because of her well-developed chest and doll-like face. "Jane Mansfield," we retort, "except that she's Jewish and has brown hair."

"Have faith," Ellen encourages. My friend often disses me for what she considers to be unnecessary worry. The truth is, I am almost wishing Leslie will strike out because I am up next. If Leslie gets on base, I'll bat with bases loaded.

From the loudspeakers on the field's perimeter, the voice of Mrs. Goldstein, the owner of the bungalow colony, announces a phone call from the central office.

"Mrs. Litwak, you have a phone call. Mrs. Litwak, phone call." Mrs. Goldstein pronounces the "W" as a "V" in a still-strong Eastern European accent.

Mrs. Litwak, Jeannette, emerges from her bungalow, her hair in curlers and a dishtowel over her shoulder. She runs quickly to the phone box some yards away, nailed into the side of the Cohens' bungalow.

Linda has one eye watching her mother standing at the phone and one eye on the field. The boys have messed up again. This time, the fault is a bad case of hormonal interference. Leslie quickly advances to first base, her long skinny legs beating out the boys' fumble. Cora runs, grabbing second base while Laurie slides into third.

"Where's the ball?" Linda screams.

Leslie's hit fell short, a sort of accidental-on-purpose bunt, just as Billy was looking toward third base, his sightline catching Laurie, his obvious crush.

Laurie is one of the cutest girls on our team. Not only do her heart-shaped face, brown ponytail, and petite nose draw Billy's eyes, but her tanned legs are distracting—and she's acting suspiciously like she's about to steal home. Richard is going noisily nuts, alerting Billy on second and Craig on third to keep a close watch.

"What the... Hey, get with it, you guys! You pantywaists! These *girls* are about to beat you!"

Richard is smarting from Billy's fumble where his distraction lost critical seconds while calculating the cost of tagging Leslie out at first or chasing Laurie to third. Finally, he runs toward third base where Laurie's foot tags the dusty bag a millisecond before his glove tags her back.

Despite his rancor, Richard's reprimands are not producing the desired effect; instead of motivating his team, his shouting appears to have sucked the wind out of the boys' sails. I can see the tender skin of their young cheeks flush red with every indictment.

"You don't have eyes in the back of your head, Bill!" Richard barks.

In the outfield, Alan Rosenblatt poses coolly, separated by twenty yards from the fray. Composed, he has nothing to be embarrassed about. He assisted in getting the ball to the infield, playing his position precisely, and executing his play efficiently. It isn't his fault the boys in the infield have grease in their gloves and eyes on their crush. In baggy khaki shorts and a white cotton T-shirt, Alan's presence distracts me dangerously.

Last night, we held hands walking in the dark under the stars from my end of the bungalow colony to his. We held hands and didn't speak much, but his hand was warm, and I was very happy. I wanted life to stop right there and then. He's my height, with straight sandy blond hair that falls in his eyes and just a few freckles around his small nose and apple cheeks. A solid frame with not an ounce of fat, he has sturdy legs and eyes like blue-green marbles. His silence wraps him in mystery. I'm a talker, but somehow, I never know what to say to him. He's the first boy I ever kissed.

"Joanie!" Linda shouts, her voice hoarse. "You're up!"

The fate of the Boys versus Girls annual baseball game resting on my shoulders, I quickly erase prurient thoughts. Nothing is more important than winning for my team, for Linda and Leslie, and Cora and Laurie. It's for my sex. Maybe, in years to come, the boys will be six-foot-tall strapping men, but this summer, we are equally built. Our team can match them inch for inch and muscle for muscle.

"Come on, Joanie!" Linda screams.

"Joanie, Joanie!" my teammates sing. The voices and sounds blur into a wave of excitement and encouragement, demand and urgency. Ten voices importuning me to win for them, ten voices counterpointed by the buzzing bees, humming cicadas, and whirring lawn mower.

I pick up a medium-weight slugger, my favorite bat from the jumble near home plate. Scuffed-up Keds firmly planted just slightly to the left of the plate, I ready my legs to run. My hands grip the bat tightly, my eyes focus on Billy winding up.

The slugger cracks with the hard contact of Billy's first pitch. To my surprise, the ball shoots past the infield, past Billy, past Scott in mid-field, and even past Alan Rosenblatt in outfield. All I hear is, "Run! Joanie! *Run*! Joanie, RUN!!!"

I have no idea where the ball is. A clutch of boys are clustered beyond second base, looking disheveled and helpless. One base after the other is wide open. I pass first, then second. Wherever the ball is, the boys are not minding their bases. Me, I'm not thinking; I'm just running as fast as hell. Apparently, it is fast enough because I'm rounding third heading for home before the ball meets the plate.

Laurie and Leslie, Cora and Linda, Ellen and Marsha are at home plate, jumping up and down and shouting my name. Linda is hugging me and everyone yells, "Joanie, Joanie!"

"You did it!" Linda shouts breathlessly.

I smile so wide, an ache cramps my cheeks. Richard, Billy, Scott, Jim, and the rest of the boys sulk off the field. All except Alan, who braves the crowd of girls to pat my shoulder. "Good work, Joanie."

Billy yells to us from a cool distance just outside the ring of kids. "You're lucky we sucked today!"

Out past the field, I see Mrs. Litwak is no longer on the phone but heading back to the bungalow. I wave and leave the pack of girls, all of us hungry for lunch, and head toward the bungalow where I am staying with Irma, my mother's best friend. My blood races with accolades, congratulations, and relief. We did it! We beat the boys. I don't want to smile, but I can't stop. As I walk down the path to the bungalow, I can't wait to tell Irma. You can't believe what happened! I'll start. Or, I did it! I hit a grand slam. Whatever. Either way, I'll get the whole story out soon enough.

When I open the door, I see the women. Sitting around the table are all of my mother's best friends: Irma, Lila, Jeanette, and Libby. I assume they are finishing up their late morning coffee klatch when Irma gets up. She puts her arm around me. "I need to talk to you," she says quietly. It's only a few steps to the small bedroom I share with Wayne and Ricky. We sit side by side on Wayne's single bed, Irma holding my hand. I don't have time to think or see the hard ball coming. "Your father has taken a turn for the worse."

She doesn't have to explain. I know. My life is about to change forever. My father is gone.

CHAPTER **1**

Hard Landing

The Bay Bridge is a composition in two-part harmony, a structural engineer's dream of an erector set pasted onto the stage set of the San Francisco Bay. The upper deck and the lower deck perform different soundtracks. The top deck: violins and soprano voices. The lower deck: basso profundo and the low woodwinds.

On one side, defining the border between Berkeley and Oakland, the Claremont Hotel is a bellwether of all things historical and proper, with its USTA tennis club, Olympic-size swimming pools, and gracious rooms. To its left, the Campanile of the University of California Berkeley is a needle piercing the soft blue sky—or, depending on your worldview, a middle finger to propriety. To the right, the Port of Oakland is a lesson in the Bay's industry: the shipping docks and the gateway to Asia. Shipping is the business that keeps San Francisco humming.

Past the Golden Gate Bridge are the Farallones; further east, between San Francisco and the cities of the East Bay, is a watery expanse that cries out for song or poetry. Gradations from green to blue to black on a body of water, dotted with white sailboats and container ships, unfolding as far as the eye can see. Mount Tamalpais in the distance is a sleeping princess, legs pouring into the sea. A wide belt of green is painted across the horizon's ridges, promising forest walks, hidden neighborhoods, and architecture that looks as if it were constructed for elves or gnomes. Not as obvious is the bay's dark side—the East Oakland I will soon get to know, the race warfare brewing and the endless "redevelopment projects" on the docket in City Hall, plans intended to restore Oakland to its former glory.

Leaving San Francisco, the lower deck is shaded but after passing through the tunnel of Treasure Island, the East Bay is revealed like a warm handshake, a gorgeous introduction to the cities perched on the edge of the continent.

Not knowing a place is like being thrust onto the set of someone else's life, all familiarity pulled like a magician pulling a cloth off a table with china and glassware. The background noises, the smells of NYC knishes, pizzas, and bakeries replaced by mussels, seaweed, and the salty bay. At the airport just moments before, watery fog wisped languidly, dreaming over a mountain crest. We leave it behind now.

Under a wide-open western sky, the bay has re-tuned me; the expanse opening my chest, the bright sun searing a film from my eyes. Where yesterday I was constrained by filthy streets and the canyon of buildings that compose the stage of NYC, here color rules: a soft blue sky and verdant rolling hills. This visual caress of mountains and islands, bridges and boats are curvilinear, a luscious, colorful Kandinsky, to New York's hard and demanding MC Escher.

The day turns dusky, and in the space between day and night, romance and expectation loiter. Shortly after exiting the bridge, Char, a friend of a friend who has generously fetched us, drives east on Ashby, turning left on Telegraph Avenue. With a flourish, she delivers us in front of Tom's apartment.

"You have arrived," Char hugs Joy.

I wave as she pulls away in her funky gray Volkswagen.

The buzzer at 2200 Durant is a strip of worn brass nubs. How many students, how many passersby, how many friends have visited this building since, as the brass placard notes, 1948? I can see parades of bobby-soxed men and women, and before them, the suited students, serious and anxious to get on to great things. Winning a spot at UC Berkeley was never easy, and once admitted, expectations were stiff. Now, though students go to school in jeans and down jackets, the look of gravitas on their faces is the same. You don't turn out more than a hundred Nobel Prize winners without putting your students through their paces, right? And a degree in pretty much anything from UC Berkeley opens doors. Doors that—I will soon see—are not so easy to open otherwise.

We press the worn brass buzzer for #23 and wait, our backpacks piled on the sidewalk like two body bags. Waiting, we discover that the street couldn't be any more entertaining! The corner of Telegraph and Durant, one block from campus, is abuzz with election night jitters. The results are coming in, and hope remains aloft for McGovern. Students scatter from last classes; the tinkling of glasses fills the streets from the sports bar and the café. Roasting meat wafts across the street from Giant Burger and a clutch of street people gather with guitars. Up the hill, a green knob calls to me. Nature! Only blocks away! My heart opens that next notch, sings that next note, and plans, plans, plans my time under redwoods and oaks.

Long brown wavy hair flows past Tom's shoulders as he flies down the stairs to greet us with a warm hug. Attractive in a studious, nerdy sort of way (glasses, narrow nose, thin lips, pale face), his build is slim. At five-foot-seven or eight, he is affable and very happy to see us. A friend of a friend of Joy's from Bard, he is a congenial Sherpa, grabbing Joy's backpack. I wave off his help, throw my backpack over my shoulders, and follow through the heavy glass door up a long flight of stained carpeted steps. My backpack knocking against my hips, Joy drags a suitcase behind her.

"US out of Vietnam!" a chorus of voices chants just below Tom's window.

"*US out of Vietnam!*" a deep male voice bellows from a megaphone.

"What do we want?"

"Freedom!"

"When do we want it?"

"*Now!*"

I lean out of the casement window, my hair quickly matted by the first rain of the season. In the short space of waiting on the street, ascending to the second floor, opening three beers, and an abbreviated getting-to-know-you chat, a protest and a rainstorm have sprung up.

"I'm going down," I announce breathlessly.

Tom lights up a joint and hands me a spare key. I rifle my backpack for a rain poncho. "We'll run across the street for a burger. Want one?"

Pulsing, I hand over a five-dollar bill. "Thanks."

I hurry down the steps, landing back at the corner of Telegraph and Durant where the protest, gathering steam, is heading toward the UC campus, a B52 whistling toward its target.

In cold November rain that now turns to a downpour, on the steps of Sproul Plaza, speakers brave the elements under umbrellas and pop-up tents to protest Nixon's policies in Vietnam and Cambodia. Frustration heats the crowd, a kettle reaching full boil. I huddle under my rain hood, surveying the dense, testosterone-stoked scene.

Nine hours ago, I was in my mother's car, heading to Kennedy Airport, after casting my first vote now that I am eighteen. I pulled down the heavy metal lever for George McGovern. Landing in San Francisco we swallowed the hard news: Nixon was ahead in the national election. Berkeley wasn't taking the sorry turn of events without a fight.

Shoulder to shoulder with the growing mob, the words shouted are angry and important but suddenly have nothing to do with my narrative. Yes, I had joined the crowds who organized to protest US involvement in Vietnam. Yes, I marched on Washington to protest the government's steady diet of lies and corporate welfare, systemized racism, and colonizing policies. I was there, raising my voice, but at this moment (to my surprise), the words aren't hitting home. Today, Nixon is not my battle.

You see, after casting my ill-fated vote, I walked directly to the newsstand to buy my first issue of *Ms. Magazine*. Buzz about a new magazine for women had been circling in the women's community for months; a magazine for women that was focused on everything other than the traditional women's magazines' "How to Please Your Man," "Fifteen-Minute Dinner Recipes," and "Beauty Tips and Diet Secrets of the Stars." Compliments of Gloria Steinem and bell hooks, we were being gifted a magazine for thinking women.

I'm not sure, but something about standing here, in the rain, with a congregation of angry men, is rendering me bereft, alone. This protest is generating a white-hot center—meaningful, direct, but whose rage frightens me.

The voices, the voluble anger coming from the top of Sproul steps, are mean and getting meaner. Men in keffiyehs roam the crowd, distributing leaflets about Israel's atrocities to Palestinians. I'm confused, getting drenched and lonelier by the minute.

I break away from the protest to rejoin Tom and Joy.

Drawn as I am to the anti-Nixon, anti-Vietnam protest, the rage fomented by a corrupt president and a meaningless war isn't what pulled me away from my mother's comfortable living room to bra burnings in Central Park. It is the familiar women's voices that admonished me to fight for the right to be myself, to throw off the yoke of male domination. Even if I do not yet know who or what that self is, I long to learn; even if I never find out, fighting for the rights of women who *do* know what they want and helping to break down barriers that keep them from succeeding buoys and inspires me.

The women's movement has ignited a new flame. It's a flame for something outside of my comfort zone, a passion for something larger, and, personally, a desire for growth and freedom.

Ms. and Gloria Steinem are making social change meaningful. The statistics don't lie: women earn forty cents to the dollar to men, and the percentage of women in positions of power, including the government, is dismal. The feminist mantle has been taken up by brilliant, committed women like Bella Abzug and Ruth Bader Ginsburg. These are my people, and they are telling me it's OK to fight for myself and for the rights of women worldwide.

* * *

ON WEDNESDAY, THE MORNING AFTER Election Day, the sun shines so brightly that the previous night's rain and protest, my endless questions, Bongo Burgers, beer, and pot seem a disjointed, poorly-directed dream. Below Tom's window, students hurry to class bathed in a late fall angled sunlight. They hurry along the same avenue where an angry river of protestors rushed just hours before.

"We're meeting Nancy Henderson today, remember?" Joy, in her self-assigned role of tour director, reminds me of today's agenda. She's sipping tea from a huge cup that looks too large for her bony hands. All industry, Joy is up, washed, and dressed in jeans and a yellow frock. Her pale, nearly translucent skin is concerning in the morning's sun. Is she ill? I have no clue, but her skin is only half as concerning as her hobbled gait. Stick thin legs look dangerously incompetent, frighteningly lacking in sturdiness to carry even her petite, brittle frame.

"Ready in half an hour," I mumble. Turning over for ten more minutes of rest, I wonder if she suffered a bout of childhood polio or was struck with rickets? Joy never divulges about her health, her fragility, or her past, nor brings attention to the childlike body hidden under studied "looks" and costumes.

Despite my delight at meeting a young friend who calls herself and her friends "woman," Joy is not the friend of my dreams, not by a long stretch. Unlike myself, she is not a rock and roll fangirl and certainly not simpatico on a heart level. While I live in my body and consider myself a sensualist who soaks up color, taste, and smell, Joy exists in a world of ideas and thoughts. But she was my ticket to California. Self-involved, she's hoping to make her mark with derivative, Jackson Pollock-like paintings and strong opinions.

Though she fashions herself an intellectual, from my point of view, Joy is less creatively thoughtful than grim, never quite getting the hang of lightheartedness. I don't know the word now, but I will later: she is *dour*. She is icy as a glacier, but she knows the right people. I get on the bus.

Joy entered my life by way of Karen, whom I met in summer school, taking the two classes that I needed to graduate high school six months early.

"I'm an artist," Joy proclaimed at our first meeting. OK. She dropped out of Bard, where her art practice consisted of laying canvas on the floor and splashing paints. She dropped out to go to California. We agreed to go together.

"I'll be back in three months," I promised my mother, who worried that I wouldn't start college. "I'll go back to Israel." I had already been accepted to Hebrew University. The promise appeased her. Now, Joy and I soak up warm November sun to meet a new friend. New York's chill behind me, everything in front. We walk the dozen blocks from Tom's apartment to the address Joy had on a crumpled paper in her pocket.

Joy is a self-styled feminist; the moniker an allowance to simply do whatever she pleases. Under the feminist maxim "The Personal Is Political," Joy, against her parents' wishes, dropped out of college to search out the women at Cal Arts. But Joy, I quickly learned, uses her feminist identity to give credence to bad behavior. Ripping my poems off the wall, commandeering our schedule, leading me around by the nose. I don't think this association will last, but I plan to stick around long enough to meet the people whose names she has collected as our first Berkeley connections. I may not love Joy, but I admire the sure way she moves through the world.

I earned street cred myself, even though I didn't know that taking off alone at seventeen to fly across the world would become my first badge of honor. I wasn't waiting for approval for a work-study semester by an elite college, or sticking out two years to earn a junior year abroad. I went to Israel. There I studied and caroused with kibbutz volunteers from around the world; Swiss, French, Japanese, and Germans worked and lived in harmony. I had love affairs with Israeli soldiers and kibbutzniks.

Joy leads the way to Derby Street, a world away from Tom's dingy digs one block from campus, smack on the busy corner of Telegraph and Durant. The verdant stretch of hills on our left, known as Tilden Park, was the Berkeley section of a wide swath of the East Bay Regional Park District. A steep path up into Claremont Canyon is visible from Telegraph. Soon, I promise, I will set out to climb. Fresh grass seems as if it had sprung up overnight (I learn later that, encouraged by the first rains, it had). The green hills, the warm sun, the blue sky, and fresh air wake up a dormant need: beauty. It is possible to live near beauty.

Stationed on the corner of Derby and Hillegass, the peaks of the roof where Nancy lives command the attention of passersby. Massive but gracious, it stands majestic, surrounded by a riot of roses: yellow, white, apricot, lavender. Roses, blooming brazenly. In November! Along the front garden's edge succulents, aloes, red-hot pokers, and a century plant cut space with thick, fleshy, and sharply serrated leaves. The garden bursts with color, yellow and purple lantana, red penstemons, bushy pyracantha—candy for any bird who drops by to munch. Pines sidle up to redwoods, oaks spread their sculpted branches in the shadow of palms.

I soon understand that the plants—some imported, some native—thrive in this particular longitude and latitude. The angle of light and the brightness nearly hurt my eyes but warm me inside.

Nancy is as welcoming as Joy is icy. A warm smile and a visage as midwestern as corn, graced with long blonde hair and a ready laugh, telegraph that Nancy doesn't take herself too seriously.

The house's entrance is cool, the living room cozy with burnished redwood paneling, mullioned windows, and a stone fireplace. The kitchen is flooded with light. I don't know Nancy yet, but this house is seductive, nothing like the cockroach-infested apartment where Joy took me to meet her Bard friends who, after college, took up residence on New York City's Upper West Side, the ones who scribbled Nancy's name on a piece of paper.

"I've been playing piano with Bonnie," Nancy tells us over a plate of eggs. While she brings us into her world of performing with the band "The Red Star Singers," I wonder at her fortitude to practice and compose while that brilliant sun shines and that green hill begs my legs to know it.

After what feels like five minutes (but according to the art deco kitchen clock has been a full hour), I stand to leave. "We should let Nancy get back to practicing," I say.

"Can I give you the short tour?" Nancy offers.

Joy is game. Good, because I am as curious as a calico cat to see what caprice lies upstairs. After perfunctory introductions to Regina, a sculptor in splattered overalls just coming in from her studio class, and Clarice, the South African academic teaching on women, rape, and sexual politics at Mills College, we continue the tour.

"There is 's room," Nancy points. We peek into her large space. Walls are the same redwood siding as the living room but painted white (a trend of the '40s and '50s that was easier to continue than reverse). Annice's room has a glassed-in porch and a cold-water sink circa 1925. The creaky staircase, the worn floors, whisper history and secrets from the time it allegedly spent as the governor's mansion. The next room is Cindy's, a ceramicist. Last is Karen's, the former model, who laughs when she says, "I'm painting, but not too seriously."

Back downstairs the living room is now in half shade, a splintered darkness that lends the room a mystery it hadn't had in full sun. Who lived here before a commune of women? I wonder aloud. "Derby Street," Nancy tells us, "is a very important house indeed!" She gives a light chuckle, and we all know what that means: in no one's imagination would the governor's mansion be occupied by eight feminists.

On the walk home, my blood vibrates with energy as if a piano is drumming fortissimo, its notes running roughshod through my veins. Apparently, permission had been granted to these beautiful women to call themselves artists. Could I, too, be granted permission, or was it simply a matter of saying, "I am. I am an artist"?

For now, I have a new friend, a warm sun, a canyon, and a hill within walking distance. And if things with Nancy go well, I will come to know a household of like-minded women. Artists.

CHAPTER 2

Cloudy with a Chance of Poetry

"What do you do?" a wiry woman stands on the top step of the Derby Street house. Her voice is the tone of a B sharp crystal bell. A helmet of blonde hair circles the inquiring woman's face so that, from a distance, a wispy, angelic halo glows around her head in the bright afternoon sun.

"I'm a poet."

I have never uttered the words in public. They simply escape as quickly as a prisoner out of her cell. *Brave*, I think, congratulating myself, *if a tad specious*. Books have been my companions since my mother took me to the library at four years old. By third grade, I was writing book reports, a love of analyzing and explaining becoming a way of moving through the world. By high school I was writing simple poems. I wasn't sure what I expected, but it was a safe place to put the feelings I didn't have the courage to speak.

Now, today, am I daring to elevate myself to poet among the ilk of my icons, Yoko Ono, Lawrence Ferlinghetti, and e. e. cummings? Nah. Not yet anyway. I could equivocate, but in this brief, sunshiny moment, "budding poet" sounds silly, "struggling poet" precious. So yes, I am a poet, even if the last thing I expected was to be shouting the words on Derby Street for any passerby to hear.

"Do you type your poems?" The woman's energy is so palpable and kinetic that I am reminded of a marionette, all thin arms and legs pulled by forces from beyond. Her face is as round as the moon.

"No," I answer, abashed. "What's your name?"

I had dropped by Derby Street to see if Nancy was around. She isn't home so I turn to leave, only to run head-on into a conversation about what "I do."

"I'm Cloud! Now go type your poems!"

And with that, Cloud disappears into the house through the heavy door, the charged air following behind like a brisk wind.

Type your poems. Is there some outside sign of my sloppy habits, my chaotic lack of organization? How could Cloud know that my "poems" are jumbled and scattered? I write, pulling words out of thin air, reporting on the explosive events around me: the kidnapping of the newspaper magnate William Randolph Hearst's granddaughter, Patty Hearst, the Symbionese Liberation Army and People's Liberation Front bombings, the jazz that has changed the way I think about music. But they are scribbles, scraps of paper in journals and notebooks, envelopes, paperbacks. If, rarely, I deemed a poem viable, if the kernel of the poem, the gem, the inspiration, actually contained the seed to bloom into something of interest, I might squirrel it away, an acorn in my special "save" pile. But saved or not saved is not the issue; *owning* "I am a poet" is not yet something I can do.

To claim myself a writer, I'll have to excavate my past, the push and pull of emotions, my disappointments, the rancor I feel toward what is left of my family, the meaningless and random sex I have both sought out as a balm, as validation of my existence, and as a way of creating the connection I am sorely missing. Better chaos and the lack of ownership than typed and open to criticism.

Less than three weeks after the chance meeting with Cloud, change comes by way of a new apartment—and with it, I begin to cotton to the idea of becoming a writer.

After Joy ripped down my poems pinned to the wall above my desk, instead of confronting her, I checked the co-op board: *Room for rent $50/month.*

My new home at 2619 Regent isn't the historic, commanding women's house at Derby Street (with its gracious common rooms, its rose garden leading up brick front steps, its dormers and hidden rooms, marble sinks in the bedrooms and glassed-in sunrooms), but it is a significant improvement over the two-room apartment I shared with Joy (with its poorly painted beige walls trying hard, and failing, to disguise nail scars, thumbtack holes, and decades of student living). 2619 Regent Street is like entering a botanical garden after sitting on a tattered bench in a city park; there is energy and light and a Cecil Bruner rose bush growing up its redwood shingled side.

Just around the corner from the women's house on Derby, 2619 Regent Street is a two-story turn-of-the-century home converted into a rooming house for students. Its front yard is ill-kempt and overgrown, but a majestic redwood tree compensates for the weeds, and the climbing rose outside of my leaded glass windows lets off a gentle, perfumed fragrance. The kitchen is dreary, the dullness exacerbated by nasty old appliances, stained linoleum, and grease-spattered walls. It isn't perfect, but no question—it is home.

The room is perfect. On a quiet street, the Bay's breezes waft through the large old windows. It is large enough for a desk, my bed, and a small altar where I can keep my crystals and pictures of the Sierras and alpine lakes. There is a wide door I can close when I want to be alone or when I am writing. A small walk-in closet is useful for extra storage. It is the first room I have had all to myself since I left home a year ago.

It lightens my mood and gives me hope of creating a life that I will carve, not under Joy's auspices or control, but on my own, with my own room.

I'm astonished about how events are unfolding, a pinch of serendipity at every turn, my life a yellow brick road: one brick to the next. So far, it's a happy path. Since being admonished to type my poems, I've diligently found and purchased a typewriter at Value Village, the go-to thrift store on San Pablo Avenue. The last weeks found me typing new poems and revising salvaged scraps.

I may be lost, unsure of where life is taking me, but one thought hounds me: I need a mentor, someone more than a friend. Maybe it's hanging around with Nancy and seeing how Bonnie has taken her under her wing, how she brought her into the Red Star Singers and helped her to become a performing musician. Maybe it's my longing for my father, my inspiration and sounding board. What comes to mind now is that I need a trusted advisor, a brave partner who has ventured down the writing road. After typing my poems these past weeks, I think that maybe Cloud, a poet and an artist with a tinkling laugh and Peter Pan body, might fit.

* * *

I WALK SOUTH ON HILLEGASS AVENUE, watching the house numbers for Cloud's address. "Come for lunch," Cloud said when I ran into her again. I was having tea with Nancy at Derby Street and she was visiting Karen, a lithe woman who worked as a high fashion model and recently came out as a lesbian.

Hillegass Avenue is lined with brown shingled houses that boast generous, lush gardens. Birds of paradise, foxglove, nasturtiums, roses of all varieties, and geraniums bloom in an enchanting mixture of shape and color. Palm trees add a tropical air to the Berkeley cityscape.

It was here that Bernard Maybeck and his protegee, Julia Morgan, launched their own unique style of architecture, a combination of the emerging Arts and Crafts school of Greene and Greene, and the classical Beaux-Arts. Julia was the first woman architect to graduate from the École des Beaux-Arts in Paris, finally overcoming the harsh admission qualifications after three rejections. But it's one thing to read about Berkeley's streetscape and another to be here. The gardens and houses exude serenity and calm and have the distinct effect of invoking a sort of amnesia; with all this beauty, I forget that I am in a world-class city (albeit a small city, but a city, nonetheless).

Over time I will come to love all that my adopted city has to offer—beside the obvious appeal of bookstores, cafés, and good cheap eats. There is the renowned Berkeley Symphony, the performing arts program at Cal that brings in international artists, the small movie theaters on Shattuck Avenue showing obscure foreign films, and the Berkeley Art Museum, a wonderful airy space with a film archive and a welcoming sculpture garden. There is a rose garden in the North Berkeley hills with bushes blooming in November, and there is also a delicious menu of culture and art, modern dance, jazz, and rock and roll.

This is not a city of hidden enclaves, secreted behind tall gates, no high hedges to keep walkers' eyes away, no long driveways with houses set back far from the street. Here, the homes are democratic, part of the streetscape: a Swiss chalet here, a country cottage there, a Spanish colonial down the street. Homeowners stage their own resistance with placards and yard signs: "US Out of Vietnam,""Oh Hell No! We

Won't Go!" "Black Power!" and "A fairy lives in this house!" The yard signs lay bare residents' proclivities, preferences, and passions. Tiny brass bells and chimes hanging from tree branches charm walkers with their magical, unpredictable notes, sung by the wind.

I ring the buzzer at the door of a small, rustic structure, half expecting an elf to greet me. Is this a garage? A chicken coop? A potting shed? Whatever it was, it's been converted to Cloud's nest.

"Welcome!" Cloud flings opens a weathered wooden door. "Perfect timing!"

My poet friend bounds up a flight of steps, clicking off a talk radio show. I feel as if I'm entering the middle of a song to which I don't know the words or the tune. "I'm a news junkie," she admits, taking my hand and leading me through the narrow hallway piled with books. "I need to know what's going on at all times," she gallops off on a diatribe about the fight for gay rights being waged in the California Senate, the trial of the Symbionese Liberation Army who had claimed responsibility for kidnapping of Patty Hearst, and the trial of three people claiming allegiance to the New World Liberation Front, implicated in the bombing of a police station.

We pass a bedroom, or at least I think it's a bedroom. Mattress on the floor, desk by the window, poems and Rapidograph drawings clipped to a clothesline running across the middle of the room. The whimsical pen drawings sway in the gentle breeze from an open window like bright, clean laundry. The drawings' lines, all thin figures with arms and legs akimbo, mirror Cloud's own—a marionette pulled by magnetic forces.

The rooms are all Cloud, all the time, her "self" commanding every corner. On the walls are posters of angels, quotations.

You have to write—even if you are sure no one will ever read it.

Drink coffee black—Balzac did!

Teach us to care and not to care. Teach us to sit still. —T. S. ELIOT

And everything comes to One, as we dance on, dance on, dance on. —THEODORE ROETHKE

Comparisons are odious. —14TH CENTURY SAYING

Every exit is an entry somewhere else. —TOM STOPPARD

Mesmerized by the room, the swaying drawings, the maxims on the wall, the books lining the bookshelves, I am interrupted by Cloud's voice.

"So happy you are here, Joan Pinecone!" Cloud christens me with what becomes my "Berkeley name," flinging open her arms like a sea bird—pelican or albatross—her wingspan that wide. "Joan Pinecone," I nod, pleased at the close rhyme and three syllable moniker that embraces my love of trees and all things green. I hug my new friend, hovering in the kitchen where she is putting the finishing touches on two plates of red leaf lettuce. Joan Pinecone, I think, enjoying the new identity. Cloud is arranging tiny cherry tomatoes, sliced almonds, curls of cucumbers and carrots and the obligatory alfalfa sprouts onto ceramic plates.

"Cheese?" she asks.

I suddenly feel shy, realizing that the lunch is the first meal anyone has prepared for me since my arrival. "Don't fuss. And yes, thank you."

"Good, good," she nods, sprinkling a small handful of fragrant sheep feta, a last dash of sunflower, and a sprinkling of black sesame seeds onto the artfully arranged salads. With the scent of the cheese, I am catapulted back to the tiny beach café on Mykonos where we ate sweet tomato and feta salads drenched in bitter olive oil.

"Just checking. Animals, you know. Some folks don't do animals."

"Do goats count? I mean it's only their milk, right?" I picture milking a goat. "No one hurt there, right?"

"Purists. Berkeley is lousy with purists," Cloud rolls her eyes: "Fruitarians, breatharians, yogis, pescatarians, vegans, and vegetarians," she sighs. Grabbing the plates like a seasoned waitress, she directs us through the room with the poems on clotheslines and out through a sliding door to a large wooden deck. In dappled light we sit at a small metal café table. Sun streams through the branches of a tall oak and a redwood tree, throwing a pattern of tiny bubbles onto the deck and table.

"The deck is sunnier in spring, but it's warm enough now, yeah?"

For my money, it's warm enough to take off our clothes and sunbathe, but on the street, people are wearing sweaters and light jackets. After all, it is January. "This feels like spring to me."

"Welcome to Berkeley," Cloud brandishes her fork like one of the three Musketeers, a mirthful smile on her face. "Bon appétit!"

For a short moment I savor the zip and ping of tomatoes and lemony dressing, cheese, and the dried fruits, the earth and sky of seeds and sprouts.

"Tell me," says Cloud, as she turns her chair to rest her feet on the banister of the deck. "Are you typing your poems?"

"Oh yes, I found the perfect typewriter."

"Tell," Cloud turns her attention back toward her half-eaten lunch. "Oops, be right back."

As Cloud disappears into the apartment, I wonder how much to share. I want to talk about leaving Joy, but I don't want to sound like a sourpuss, already complaining at our first meeting.

My host returns with a small basket. "Sourdough. The best! You know Morning Dew Bakery?" She doesn't wait for my answer before dipping a crust into a small dish of olive oil. I follow suit. The flavors, both bitter from the oil and sweet from the bread, remind me of Corfu, where everyone was named Spiro and we ate moussaka every day in the tavernas. In a short moment of silence, I become disoriented: Where am I? Italy? Greece? Sicily? The flavors and this deck, snug up to the trees, is a place to which I've never traveled. It's enticing, seductive, and very, very magical.

"Back to your poems." Cloud smiles a benevolent smile, not unlike the face on one of her angel posters. I don't know that I've ever been looked upon quite this kindly. Maybe by Mrs. Lacey, my fourth-grade teacher and my biggest fan. Maybe by my grandmother, once or twice when not fretting over her pot roast or scrubbing her floors. Friends have smiled at me, yes, but there is a quality of receptivity in Cloud's eyes that shift something in me. A door creaks open, and suddenly I want to tell her everything. About my shyness as a poet, about Joy, about my room and how the roses scratch at the window on windy nights, about finding the guy who sold me a bamboo flute, about my walks in Strawberry Canyon with Nancy. About the yellow brick road and everything feeling destined, fated, important.

But I begin by telling her about the provenance of the typewriter. "An old S electric. I paid for a desk too."

I tell Cloud how I left Joy, sparing her details about Joy's rigidity and controlling behavior, and I tell her about settling in at Regent Street and the characters I have met there. (I keep the story of my one-night stand with a guy who sold handmade guitars on Telegraph to myself. Drawn in by a handsome handmade flute, we'd struck up a conversation. I could not resist his long burnished red hair, delicate hands, and long piano-playing fingers.)

"I met Joy in New York. She seemed cool, dropping out of Bard to come to California to be a painter. I was sold when she told me that she had a couple of friends here, but she turned out to be a buzzkill! She took my poems down off the wall over my desk when I was away."

"Deal breaker!" pronounces Cloud, her face screwed up into a pout. "Definite deal breaker." After nonstop moving since I arrived,

Cloud relaxes, her eyes meet my eyes. "What sign are you?" She squints, as if she could guess.

"Libra. And you?"

"Oh my god, I knew it! Gemini. Libra and Gemini are famous as friends! John Lennon and Paul McCartney."

We clink water glasses. "To Libras and Geminis!"

"So what are you up to, what do you want?" she says. "I'm all about alchemy by the way. I think there is a reason you are in Berkeley, Joan Pinecone."

"Alchemy?"

I'm glad to have Cloud's focus off of myself for a moment. I don't relish interrogations, especially now, when I'm not sure what I'm doing. I like her enthusiasm—and, honestly, I'm basking in her warm glow, but I'm not sure that I have answers to her questions.

"Poetry is alchemy, music is alchemy. It's the casting of spells. It is witchcraft in a technical sense, but it's also a combination of elusive, mysterious elements that makes art, relationships, and music work. The formal definition," here, Cloud stands up, "a seemingly magical process of transformation, creation of combination."

"Like your salad here?"

Cloud lets loose a joyful huzzah. "You get it!"

A welcome moment of silence is broken by stellar jays squawking, squirrels muttering, and neighborhood dogs yapping.

"What do you want?" Cloud asks directly.

"What do I want?" I ask, my heart skipping a beat. The innocent question hits me like a landmine. Finding myself at the mouth of a cave—there's light there but it only goes as far as the opening.

"Yeah."

"I want to write," I say warily. "I came to Berkeley for a stopover. I had plans."

"Had plans?" Cloud jumps in, putting "had" in air quotes.

Something about her bemused and kindly tone suggests futility. What else would I want to be doing but being here, *now?* And at this moment, on this deck, in this warm sun, with Cloud and her beautiful salad…I see her point, if that is her point. "…To go back to live in Israel," I say. I remember walking in Eilat, munching on sunflower seeds with the two Moroccan-Israeli soldiers. An ache pulls. I had gone to Israel with so much…hope. "Now, I'm not sure. I enrolled in the winter semester at Laney. After that, if I still want to go back, I can try next year."

"Israel? What was that about?" Cloud tips her chair onto the back two legs, balancing her feet on the redwood railing, and turns her face up toward the sun. "Don't mind me! I haven't been outside for days—just soaking up my vitamin D." She turns, flashing a Cheshire cat smile. "I'm listening!"

"Yeah, I know—the Promised Land right? I think the name might be too 1945." I stop myself, rein in the glib. "I was taken in by kibbutz life. It's the grand Socialist experiment! Farming in a community peopled by European intellects. How much better could life get than living in nature, working in orchards, and discussing books, poetry, and opera?"

"But…?" Cloud hums.

"But early on I saw discrimination against Jews who were not European. Can you believe that?" I pose rhetorically. "I just saw a sad repeat of the states: Black versus white and all that. I lost heart." The rush of anger that surged when I learned about how dark Jews were relegated to second-class citizenship returns. "Been there, done that, right?" I stand, talking to Cloud's blonde helmet of hair. "My father prayed in a synagogue with Black Jews. I have no truck with Israeli elitism." I think back to the Moroccan soldiers who explained that second-class citizens or not, they were required to serve army time just like everyone else. What I don't tell Cloud is that when I returned to New York, I was disappointed, sad, my dream of an even-handed Jewish homeland dashed. And so, I moved my Jewish identity down the list, abandoning the idea that being Jewish was "the answer" for how I fit in to the world. Now I'm less certain about my identity, sure, but I'm starting to get hints.

"Here, I'm meeting artists. Nancy, you know from Derby Street, and there's Jake, a musician who lives in the attic of my house. There's Bonnie, and now, you. I've been going to readings and concerts almost every night."

Cloud tips her chair back now, all four legs securely on the redwood deck. "Do you mind if I clear the table? We'll have tea."

As Cloud busies herself in the kitchen, I have a sense that here I could not only become part of a community as I had in Israel, but at the same time, I could incorporate my whole self, not simply be a cog to keep the wheel of the kibbutz turning, writing in secret, my sense of myself wobbly. Here, in the sympathetic environment that is the women's art community, I have been given credence to find my voice, however slowly, however wobbly. Here is not only the "all for one and one for all" attitude of kibbutz life but an "all for one and one for myself" attitude that, honestly, I'll need if I am going to become a writer. And while I loved being a part of the community in Israel, I see now that autonomy was the missing ingredient. That getting up at five to pick oranges and grapefruits in the winter, then pears and avocados in the summer, each day chained to a schedule of working and meals, might not be the most conducive to poetry. And that living in a young country whose survival and safety takes precedence over personal happiness, while thrilling and purposeful, might not be the best recipe to bring my shy, tentative writing to fruition.

Cloud returns with two mismatched cups of steaming rosehip tea, disappears back inside, and brings a plate of butter cookies. "Sounds to me like what you want is to write." Cloud tips her chair back again, rearing on the two back legs.

"I think so."

"Seriously?"

"Seriously."

Beyond the deck, in the shady backyard, a tiny iridescent hummingbird pushes its beak into a pink and red fuchsia blossom. Its green back shimmers in the afternoon sun, wings flap insanely fast—the *whrrrr* sound more like a buzzing mosquito than a bird. Cloud's nurturing lunch and innocent inquiry has lit a flame inside. I'm relaxed and buzzing, as if we had smoked a joint of really good pot.

"This could be home," I start.

Cloud turns her moon face toward the sun.

"Before I left New York, I had a dream." I walk to face Cloud, not wanting to share an intimacy with the top of her head. She looks up, focused. "I was in a forest looking up at a gigantic redwood tree. I fell to my knees, awed by its size and power. I'd never seen a redwood tree in my life."

"Write that!" Cloud exhorts from her sunny spot.

Beyond the reach of the deck, chickadees, nuthatches, an elusive goldfinch, and an owl counterpoint silent fluttering of yellow and orange butterflies appearing and disappearing in the high branches of oaks and redwoods. I gather my things. Beside an aversion to overstaying my welcome, I'm inspired to go home and write.

I leave Cloud's glowing. It wasn't just the vegetables that tasted hand-picked, or the warm sun, or even Cloud's corroboration that Joy's removal of my poems was a "deal breaker." It is, as Cloud said, the alchemy. As if our meeting had been predestined, as if the room with her poems pinned to a clothesline were my own, as if the deck and the swallowtails and monarchs are as important to the sun, the air.

Everything about our meeting was inspired, so different from a first meeting of awkward attempts searching for common ground.

Reversing my steps to Regent Street, I notice little. What vibrates is this: Cloud acknowledged me both for who I am now and who I aspire to be. I'm not just an object of sexual desire or a silly girl wanting to be a poet. After a youth where validation from boys was the currency, this is a first. "I want to go to art school," I told my mother on a quiet, snowy afternoon. She was teaching me to paint with acrylics on tiles. "You? You can't even draw a straight line." That settled that. Take guitar lessons, painting lessons, or horseback riding? No time, no money, and besides, I didn't have the talent for it.

Cloud, with her laissez-faire attitude, her sunny optimism, and her curiosity has peeled back a layer of skin to uncover my real self. There are still layers beneath, but even this layer isn't one I easily reveal.

Meeting Sonya

Tuesday night. "Women's Night" at the White Horse, a gay bar just over the Oakland border on Telegraph Avenue and Alcatraz. Karen, Jake, Nancy, and I are the only ones who were game, so off we drove in the Cherry Bomb, the moniker of my 1963 red Dodge Dart.

Jake runs into Linda Tillery, a drummer, and Karen gets pulled into a hug by Jane, a butch woman who has been pursuing her for the past month. Despite protestations, Karen looks pretty cozy in Jane's embrace, her arm possessively around her waist. I head for the dance floor. The upbeat rhythms of "Soul Train" are an invitation to move.

After a few dances alone, I'm leaning against a wall and sipping a Pacifico beer. I notice a dark-haired, voluptuous woman dancing with a thin blond with slim hips. Is it Earth, Wind & Fire or the Temptations that the DJ is spinning? Whoever it is, it has a beat, and under the disco ball's shards of white light, I lose myself in the collective body heat, our minds blissfully, if only for the moment, blank.

I dance—intermittently quaffing Pacifico from the bottle, my tastebuds parsing the bitter from the sweet, the hops from the yeast—

and surreptitiously survey the scene. I'm still a bit jittery from the police stop on the way over.

"Yes, officer," I complied, all business, my friends snickering in the back seat.

"License, registration."

All was in order, but the wait seemed endless. Did I run a red light? I knew Cherry Bomb had a broken left turn signal, but I had turned right. Was a taillight busted? A brake light off? We were quiet, waiting as if for a verdict in court. The minutes ticked, and even though it was a cool forty-degree night, a thin bead of sweat formed on my scalp.

The officer returned with my license and registration. "All good," he said.

"What the fuck was that about?" I asked the group, cautiously driving away.

"They probably think we are harboring Patty Hearst, or a group of terrorists. You know these Berkeley beats, they took lessons from the Keystone Cops," Karen said blithely.

Everyone laughed nervously, but I was shaken. Terrorists?

The DJ switches from soul music to "Saturday Night Fever." My heart picks up speed, and my feet itch. I ditch my flannel overshirt and dive onto the dance floor.

I abandon myself to the beat, to pulsing light, and to mindlessness. Who said there wasn't a "there there" in Oakland? (Yes, yes, Gertrude, I know.) Well, perhaps in 1910 there was no *there there*, but this night, this bar, these people are the exact center of the universe, the beating heart of change. Here, at Telegraph and Alcatraz, we stand at ground zero of a social and political cataclysm.

The Bay Area may not have the architecture and history of Paris or New York, but a new history is being written daily. I am in a maelstrom, a tornado of energy that has invigorated the city with hope and pride, dignity and rights. Like salt from a shaker, spiritual seekers, Deadheads, politicos, poets, scientists, philosophers, and dreamers arrive in Berkeley by the caravan, by VW vans, by train and airplane. San Francisco is suffering the aftermath of an influx of hippies; the Haight Ashbury is a shadow of its former self, a war zone of shuttered storefronts, burnt-out druggies, and bedraggled latecomers searching for the Summer of Love. Market Street, the central artery of the city, is torn up for Bay Area Rapid Transport (BART). Berkeley is a safe haven for misfits and outcasts, for rebels and thinkers who no longer feel at a home in their hometowns. San Francisco has become a safe harbor for gay men, but Berkeley is where the women gather, close to those verdant hills where we can hike and garden.

Women have emerged from the complacency of the 1950s. Now, post–Civil Rights, we are protesting male-dominated political dialectics. Even the privileged heiress Patty Hearst rejected her family's money and power, donned a machine gun and beret, and brought the world's attention to class, entitlement, white privilege, and the imperative to take care of our poor. "The personal is political" is the mantra, the clarion call to women breaking out of confining roles, reinventing every institution from families to food. Nuclear families are morphing into communities, groups are living together to create support networks.

Women-only bands are signing contracts with women-owned record companies; women's books are being published by women's presses; women's film openings feature films directed and written by women. Women-only clinics, women's shelters, women's bookstores, and women's cafés are sprouting up all over the Bay Area. Women are creating spaces to find their voice, whether to excel in art, music, feminist theory, or banging a hammer. Women work together with men as long as they are on their side, as long as they can relinquish their expectations of women as caretakers, baby makers.

For myself, any struggle I'm going to fight must reach beyond myself to building a better, more sustainable, and just world. Maybe it was my father's influence, and his love for *tikkun olam* (repairing the shards of the broken world), but I was indoctrinated in this Jewish precept.

When "How Deep Is Your Love" ends, I wipe my forehead with the fringe of my T-shirt. And there is that dark-haired woman, her arm around my arm, inviting me for the next dance. For this moment, it doesn't matter who I am, who she is, who Jake is, or Karen, or anyone. Women's night is about loud music, beer drinking, bodies, and rhythm.

The DJ slows down the crowd with Elton John's "Your Song." I take the dark woman's hand and steer her toward an open seat at the fireplace. I have to find out about this goddess who looks descended directly from Judith. This woman who is a Rubenesque beauty with an aristocratic nose, violet eyes, and a mane of black curls. If I squint just slightly, I can see the biblical Jewish stunner, now with a devilish sparkle in her eyes.

I am about to offer to buy her a beer when she kisses me, deep and sweet.

"Whew. And who are you?" I ask, dropping into an open chair for support.

"I'm Sonya. I'm a jeweler."

"Tell me more."

"I learned jewelry making in India," she starts. "I bought a supply of beads and silver to start my own business."

I am intrigued. Sonya explains that the affordable prices allowed her to set up shop on Telegraph Avenue. "I have enough for at least a year."

"Then what?" The DJ spins "Ain't No Mountain High Enough," and I'm tempted to cajole Sonya back to the dance floor, but I want to hear the rest of her plan.

"After that, I'll figure it out. I'll either make enough money to go back to India or I'll do something else."

Listening to Sonya, I hear a kindred spirit: a woman whose fate is tied to no one but herself, who without protection or guidance has figured a way to live a good life in Berkeley. Listening to the tone of her voice, to the depth of her tone, to her determination and confidence, I hear my mother tongue. Her voice is familiar and comforting. I can hear my hard-working seamstress grandmother. Not every voice sounds as if it's been handed down from one hundred generations. Many of my Jewish friends descended from European stock, but their voices don't resonate with Sonya's ineffable intonation. I'm in the White Horse Bar, sipping a Pacifico beer, but I'm also a time traveler, racing back to the Negev, to the Sinai, to that well where the women—my foremothers Sarah, Rebecca, Rachel, and Leah—met and planned.

I have the sense of knowing Sonya from somewhere. I feel safe. I'm listening to tales of India, Morocco, and Spain, loving the way Sonya moves through the world, creative, adventurous, humble.

"I have an early morning," she reports, grabbing her jacket from a hook. "Come see me. My booth is between Channing and Durant," she turns toward the open door. "I like you."

At home that night, I light a votive candle I picked up at Crystal Way. The word "Affirmations" is printed in purple around the light's circumference.

Despite the bar's loud music still buzzing in my ears, Sonya's beauty is blazoned in my mind's eye. I arrange my zafu in front of the makeshift altar. With a light tap of a wooden mallet, I ring the brass bell for a short night meditation. The house and the street outside are blessedly quiet. I surrender to silence.

Meditation brings a sense of sloughing off one set of assumptions, plans, and dreams while preparing my skin, my body, for another. Meeting Sonya might or might not be a sign that I can explore who I will be while holding on to my Jewish roots. By living her uncharted path, Sonya inspires me. She's the first woman entrepreneur I've met. I'm intrigued.

And so, change is possible; a person's identity can shift. It might require effort, confidence, and direction, but it is possible. When I flew on that 747 from JFK to Tel Aviv, I was convinced that my identity as a returning Jew was *bashert*, fated. As the Hasidim *davened* in the aisles at daybreak, I truly felt that I was going home. But since I arrived in Berkeley, a tectonic shift has rearranged the plates under my feet. It's as if my cells are re-ordering, my skin regrowing. I've left behind every part of me but my passion for the written word, art, and music. I cast off my identity as caretaking daughter, sister, niece, and granddaughter when I joined my Berkeley tribe.

Drifting to sleep I consider the advantage of having a mother whose sole focus was struggling to survive. Unlike other daughters and women of my age, my mother did not burden me with expectations nor the baggage of parental prescriptions. Yes, my mother expected me to go to college, but she never specified where.

And although she tried every trick to talk me out of leaving home and cried bitter tears when I told her of my plan, she capitulated. If my mother wasn't so fragile, maybe she would have made the same decision to leave her home. And, giving her the benefit of the doubt, she knows me well enough to know that I'm a serious person; I'm not going on a years-long vacation. I'm on a mission.

I think of how Sonya and I hadn't asked each other anything about our histories. Because in Berkeley, nothing about our pasts matters.

Nothing about Peoria, Normal, Detroit, Chicago, Paris, New York, Redondo Beach, or even San Diego matters. What matters is that we are here, together, building a world that can support us in all our complexity.

The time spent in Israel was not lost; living in a country of Jews, close to the land and with thousands of years of history, marked my soul. I circle back to my first thought after meditation: Can identities shift and shed, or do they compound? Do identities grow to form a patchwork, leaving a person imprinted with life lessons that she can tap into? Here, a piece of me, Jewish. There, a piece of me, daughter. There, poet. Here, lover; there, friend. I don't have to choose, I tell myself. And with that simple insight, I am comforted.

CHAPTER **4**

Worst Thanksgiving Ever (1967)

Grey as dirty dishwater, the sky shivers over New York like a sad, used-up dishrag. Even the rainclouds are crushed. Dawning cold and hopeless, the day, against its better judgement (it is a national holiday after all), gets worse, not better. After hours of reading Chaim Potok's *The Chosen*, I need to leave the four walls of my room, get away from the dirty window looking out over the concrete courtyard. Fresh air (even if it is damp, cold, November air) might lighten my anxiety. I'm unsettled about the sad day my mother has planned: today of all days! Apart from family, the three of us will eat Thanksgiving alone in our small kitchen. The plan feels like a punishment, salt in the wounds, and a slap in the face all at once.

"I'm going out," I yell from the hall.

My mother sits at the kitchen table, poring over recipes for roast duck.

"Be back by three," she says, not looking up. Cigarette smoke fills the kitchen.

Bundled up warmly in my wool winter coat, thick scarf, and gloves, I cautiously cross the scary six lanes of Queens Boulevard (from our "new side" of Forest Hills to the "old side") where the doctors, lawyers, and old money reside. "Old Forest Hills" is where residents play at the Forest Hills Tennis Stadium; where neighbors gather for tea and cocktails, card games, and backgammon; and where kids carefreely roam the streets on bikes. I've called Vivian for a walk. In the only bright spot of today, she said yes.

Walking toward Austin Street, I am sad: Why can't my mother plan a normal Thanksgiving? She's cooked a turkey before (or has she?), opened cans of cranberry sauce, bought and baked pans of stuffing. Her "sweet potato pie" is a quickie: candied yams from a can, covered with puffy marshmallows and baked. Easy, right? I'd even take a large chicken! But a duck? My mother, whose one claim to culinary fame is beef stew in a pressure cooker? The dish requires all of two steps: cubing meat and slicing red peppers. The only reason I can think for the self-isolation, the cooking on her own, the "branching out" gastronomically, is that this is her way of telegraphing to the family—to her brother who worries about her nonstop (he calls me nightly to see how she is doing) and to grandma, her mother-in-law who is her rock—that she is capable, that she can take care of her little family herself.

I'm thirteen; too young to make my own plans and too old to sit around watching the Macy's Thanksgiving Day Parade and cartoons all day. The idea of all that bright joy, the oversized balloons of Disney characters and Christmas ornaments, that manic festivity, leaves me bereft.

Besides, I'm at an awkward age, a confusing age, an age where even if I wasn't navigating life as a fatherless child, I still wouldn't know which way was up; thirteen is just confusing. "Girl or boy?" the grocery checkout clerk teases when I shop. I'm at that ambiguous age, part tomboy, part budding adolescent. Curious about sex, but shy and unsure whether snuggling in bed with my upstairs neighbor, Clare, is normal or weird. The clerk's comment kicks a hole in the thick wall I've built around myself, a wall I need to hide behind to protect my standing as a weirdo without a father and normal family, child of a mother hanging on by a thread and who can barely get out of bed. And now, we can't even have a normal Thanksgiving?

The walk with Vivian through Old Forest Hills produces the opposite of my intention; instead of making me feel better, it makes me feel worse. Kicking piles of dead leaves, I get caught up and sadder by the enticing smell of fireplace smoke pouring out of chimneys where families gather in front of open drapes, with cocktails and canapes, with grandma and grandpa, mother, father, cousins, and babies. I'm so sad that I can't find words to make conversation with my best school friend. Waving goodbye, I head toward the dreaded meal at home, the outing leaving me locked deeper inside myself than when I left.

The table is set for a normal day. Chipped dinner dishes, water glasses, paper napkins. No fancy silverware, no china. On the table, a dead duck reposes in a greasy roasting pan; a green salad of iceberg lettuce, hot house tomatoes, and tasteless cucumber winks in a wooden bowl; a new bottle of Thousand Island dressing standing sturdy like the savior it is; and, in at least a nod to a normal Thanksgiving, a sweet potato pie. As much as I'm ambivalent about my grandmother, I miss her in this moment. At least grandma can cook.

Unceremoniously, my mother, who apparently has forgotten to change out of her housedress, attacks the duck with a sharp knife. She places two slices on each of our plates and we silently fall to eating—or, rather, we try to.

I pick up my knife, but it refuses to cut the meat. "It's rubbery," I whine, taking a bite of sugary sweet potato pie as consolation.

"Try another piece," my mother removes the offending piece from my plate, switching it for one of her pieces.

"Mine too," my older sister, Rachelle, says quietly, her knife and fork fighting with the pieces on her plate.

We fight with our rubbery, inedible meat for what seems like forever. Outside, the sky has gone from grey to black, and our collective mood downgrades to match it.

I give up the fight, push the rubbery duck to the side, and eat my sweet potato pie.

"I'm finished," I say, getting up to head back to my room.

My mother, unapologetic for this train wreck of a meal, yells after me.

"Want to…" she's asking me a question, but I am sick to my stomach. The sweet potato pie sits like a lump, and if I don't lie down, I'm afraid I'll throw up. I hear my mother lighting up a cigarette as my sister trails behind me, heading to her room down the hall.

I shut the door to my room, turning on the portable radio that has been keeping me company. Listening to The Beach Boys, The Mamas & the Papas, the Four Tops, and The Monkees, I am transported out of this sad place, my mood shifting from grey and cloudy to bright and sunny. Music touches every nerve in my body and lights it up; it is my go-to, my escape.

I remember when my father brought home the portable record player. I went nuts dancing to "The Monster Mash" in the bedroom I shared with my sister. Then he brought us *Meet the Beatles!* Life was good! Music was my happy place. Music, the light. Music, the mood shifter, uplifter. Now, I stare at the ceiling trying to parse the botched dinner. I am always one to make the best of any situation: rent collecting on the dirty lower east side? It'll be an opportunity to watch the parade of New Yorkers rushing. Stuck in a boring classroom with kids who can't read at my level? I'll read so many books that I'll win the class prize in Mrs. Lacey's fourth grade reading contest. But I can't think of one silver lining for this day.

We've just marked a year since my father passed. My mother's emotional needle has not shifted from despair and afternoon sobbing, and she is still not working. She hides out in her bedroom, sitting at the kitchen table when she wants to make a show of being strong, smoking cigarettes and drinking black coffee. I am the grocery shopper, the cleaner, and the emotional support dog. My mother is a lost ghost.

I'm in my bedroom, thinking about music and how I am going to cope with the grim atmosphere of the place I call home for another four years, when I overhear my mother and sister shouting in the hallway.

"Why did you make that disgusting dinner?" my sister is crying at my mother's bedroom door.

"The hell with you! I tried to make it nice!" my mother retorts, her voice thin with rage.

"But you don't know how to cook a duck! We couldn't eat it! I'm starving!"

I go to my door, wondering if I need to intervene, or if maybe a pizza might be on the way. I hear my mother get up out of bed, I hear the squeak of the metal bedframe. Next thing I hear is a slap. "You bitch!" my mother rails.

My sister retorts: "Get out of fucking bed! Stop smoking! Get a life!" my sister slams my mother's bedroom door.

I slink out of sight, as intuition reports that this fight has just begun. I've heard my parents fight with my sister (both of my parents are famously impatient and yellers to boot), but I've never heard my mother say the word "bitch," nor have I heard this level of blunt anger.

The voices quiet, everyone returns to their rooms like boxers to their corners, and I'm two steps away from lying back on my bed with my book and my portable radio when I hear my mother crash into my sister's room: "Then why didn't you help me?" my mother screams. "You could have pitched in."

"You never asked!"

The yelling reaches a fevered pitch. I slip under my covers, cram a pillow over my head. Could this day get any worse? Muffled screams, and more slaps. I slip out again, on patrol if things escalate. I'm opening my bedroom door, planning how to break up this futile fight, when my mother shouts, "Who gives a shit about Thanksgiving? Thanks? Yeah, thanks for killing your father!" Slap.

Now she's going below the belt. Now she's slinging some serious shit, jumping into dangerous territory. Yes, it was true, my sister had a knack for getting my father's ire up. After lobbying for a phone in her room and her own line for over a year, she would yak on the phone incessantly instead of doing homework. And at seven, with undiagnosed dyslexia, she refused to read, tell time, or write a proper school paper. The fights were epic.

"No, I didn't kill my father! Don't blame me!" my sister is shouting.

With trepidation, I step back to my doorway. "No one killed anyone," I yell, quickly pulling my hysterical mother into her room and away from my sister. Though I can't say I ever felt a deep communion with my mother, things had changed. Now, she was my only shield between having a home and orphanhood. It was a weak shield, but it was all I had. I had taken it upon myself to watch out for her, care for her, not cause her any more trouble than she already had. It was a big load for a thirteen-year-old, but who else was up to the task?

CHAPTER 5

The Portrait

Too long a source of shame and embarrassment, my breasts set me apart when, as a thirteen-year-old, they exploded from an A to a C cup. One minute, I was snug in a stretchy white training bra, the next, strapped into an adult contraption. I was horrified.

Simply walking the New York streets was an invitation to cat calls and unabashed ogling. Middle school boys only wanted to touch them. Summers were hell. Not sure where to hide and unwilling to eschew swimming, sports, or any other fun summer activity, I pulled a loose T-shirt over my bathing suit. I wasn't safe on the streets. I wasn't even safe at home. "Melons!" my sister taunted. "Casabas!"

I was learning about my body, and not in a good way. "My hips bump out," I complained to my mother.

"You have a woman's body. Enjoy it."

Enjoy it? My mother's simplistic explanation was no help. How could I enjoy it when all my friends were as thin as pencils? Couldn't my mother see that looking like a woman when my friends still looked like girls set me apart, made me self-conscious and sad? I did what I could. I built a wall of defense around myself. No eye contact, no flirting back, avoidance when possible. I was not ready for my child-hood to slip away, not yet. Already, my face was serious, my brows knit with focused concentration. And now I had to contend with a woman's body?

This is all to say that when Annice, one of the painters among the multi-talented artists at Derby Street, asks to paint my portrait— not just my face, but my full body—my first response is, "Thanks. But no thanks."

Annice found me one night at a Derby Street party, swaying alone in front of the band. In a bold move, she circled her arms around my waist, swayed with me. She was cute. The next thing I knew we were making out under the staircase. Jane is her given name, but she took Annice when she arrived in Berkeley, after Anaïs Nin. Annice is short, round, loquacious, lusty. Her Italian roots are deep, and she expresses herself with food and thickly painted canvases.

Wouldn't an artist want to paint a beautiful woman, svelte with teacup breasts like Rembrandt or Matisse? Wouldn't the artist be compelled by classic beauty, something I can never own? The thought of being immortalized in oil on canvas is far out of my comfort zone. Between my melon-sized breasts and my perennial struggle with weight, I call a day "lucky" when I am content with being cute. But Annice isn't taking no for an answer.

"Why me?"

"You're interesting looking. Mysterious. A little Jacqueline Bisset, a little Janis Joplin. Your face has depth." I guess the knitted brow is rare for an eighteen-year-old. I wonder if she can see the sadness, the confusion, the broken thing that I am.

I prevaricate. "Can we talk about this in a while? Like next year?"

Annice laughs her hearty, throaty Italian laugh. "We can talk about it. But how about next week?"

The Portrait

A week passes. Between biking to class down Telegraph Avenue, writing poems, and running around San Francisco with Jake to gay bars and music clubs, thoughts about the portrait sitting rise up and fall away, as challenging to balance as an acrobat holding an umbrella on a highwire: It's the chance of a lifetime! It will be an embarrassment! Sitting for a portrait will finally give me time to appreciate my body as a painter does, its curves and lines a thing of aesthetic interest, if not beauty. I cannot face being considered, scrutinized, and examined!

In truth, I am just beginning to make friends with my mind, to trust the words that I am writing, to trust the new ways that I am looking at the world. But I have not yet met the challenge of befriending my body, the body that has shocked and embarrassed me, the body that I haven't felt at home in since I became conscious of it.

Annice and I arrange for me to stay at her place tonight and discuss the sitting.

I am in a joyous mood. Everything about the day so far had been an affirmation of women's power, starting with breakfast at the woman-owned Brick Hut Café with Jake, a small café at the intersection of Ashby and Shattuck Avenues filled with women's art. Lesbian waitresses and cooks ran the place like clockwork.

After the marches in early 1972, inspired by Betty Friedan's *The Feminine Mystique* in New York, Washington, and Detroit, and the national "Women's Strike," the "second wave of feminism" is on solid ground with women across the country instituting changes in the home, in reproductive rights, and in the workplace. Entire communities of women are separating from the homogeneous culture to create "women's spaces." At Brick Hut Café I thought back to when I was nine, when women and girls were not allowed to wear pants to school or work, were banned from male-only clubs. Although Title IX—a law that requires businesses to have equal numbers of women employees and allow women equal access to sports and athletic schol-arships—is still being put into place, many women are impatient to get on more quickly with their liberation. Women-only spaces give women access that has been heretofore denied.

Living with only a mother and a sister from the age of twelve, I have firsthand experience with a women-only household, but these Berkeley women are tigers of another stripe! They are empowered women, women living their best lives, women thriving, not house-wives bickering and taunting and judging one another.

They are women who want it all: meaningful professions, liveli-hoods that are not soul-crushing, and they want to make a difference.

Best of all, they want fun, and they work hard and long to build community. These are women supporting other women in their artistic, political, and intellectual pursuits. The difference in attitude has opened doors I never knew existed, doors that open to a person who yearns to form and lead community, write poems, and talk about books and writers. It is a freedom and openness of which I haven't even dreamed. Liberated from the mantle of grief and insecurity? Honoring my body, my desires, my soul? Is it possible?

After breakfast, I met with Cloud at her woodsy cottage to go over recent poems. Buoyed by her enthusiasm for my new piece, "Rolling," about Patty Hearst, I headed home to read *The Mandarins* by Simone de Beauvoir and review the stack of poems sent to me, "Poetry Editor: *Plexus*."

I was offered the esteemed position of volunteer editor for the magazine. I am proud to be an arbiter of culture, listening for the next talented voice in poetry. It is inspiring and empowering and an opportunity that touches me; I have garnered the editor's trust. I have made an impression. I am one of the gang, the tribe, the community of writers and artists, newsmakers and doers!

Sipping wine in Annice's room now, I share a line from "Rolling."

"'Heads rolled. Cameras rolled. I clapped. You were getting back.'"

I quietly hope that Annice doesn't take it as an affront or believe that I am casting doubt on her competence as a painter if I say no to having my portrait painted.

"I'm shy," I tell her.

"There's nothing to be shy about. You're beautiful."

Beautiful? Then why is the thought of sitting naked in front of Annice and her painting partner giving me hives?

The conversation veers from portrait sitting and body shame to how partners try to know one another. "My ideal partner knows me without explanation," I conjecture.

"Ridiculous," Annice chides. She's frustrated.

"Why is it ridiculous to expect a partner to intuit who I am? Why does everything have to be spoken?"

"Because we don't even know ourselves. How could we deign to know someone else?" Annice counters.

I stand my ground. I am sure they are out there. Someone with whom I will be known and seen. Didn't my father see me when he peeked into my room at night? Writing a book report for school, or doing homework, I looked up to see my giant of a father, *kvelling*. I warmed with joy when he kissed my head. We didn't need words.

Annice is done with words for now too, pulling me gently to lie beside her.

The next morning, lying in bed in the glassed-in sun porch, the windows are frosted over, an exclamation point to the chill. Annice pulls an art book from the shelf.

The pages are of artists I have never seen in my New York museum haunts: Artemisia Gentileschi, Mary Cassatt, Käthe Kollwitz. How many afternoons did I hop the "F" train or the "RR" to 53rd and 5th to wander the galleries at the Museum of Modern Art (MOMA) or the Metropolitan! Why did I never discover these women artists?

Annice turns the pages as a new world opens. I fall in love with the strength, boldness, and directness of the images: the chiaroscuro of Gentileschi, the Renaissance painter; the tender mother-daughter imagery of Cassatt; Kollwitz's bold, black charcoals of war and grief.

"Are you ready?" Annice is getting ready for work.

"I'm lost in this book!"

"You can get lost in the book later—take it! What I want to know is: are you ready for your portrait? You will be a great model." Annice pulls on a white wool turtleneck, tracing my cheekbone with her soft fingers. "Come on! It will be fun."

"Okay." Under gentle pressure, I acquiesce. What could be so bad?

Watching Annice slip into her warm wool coat, I pose one last question.

"Why me?" I ask, sitting up and pulling on a grey REI fleece. "Karen," I conjure the image of the ex-model and Derby Street beauty queen, "is so pretty! And Cloud—she's a character."

"Why you? Because there's something on the surface and something hidden in you. I don't know yet what it is. I think maybe if I paint you, I will understand."

Well, Berkeley is a new life and a new place and I'm making new friends—some of whom, apparently, actually like looking at me. Who didn't call me "ugly" or my breasts "casabas."

"Painful," I say, "but I'll do it."

Annice laughs, plants a kiss on my head, and waves goodbye. Outside, the sun is just melting the icy frost that has stiffened the grass.

I organize myself to leave, slipping out without a visit to the living room where Louise and Karen drink coffee. Buried in the *Chronicle*, they barely notice as I quietly open the heavy door and step out into the bright, chilly November morning.

Last night, Annice asked, "Who are you? Where is your family?"

The question pierced; my stomach flipped inside out. I was paralyzed. No words. In six months in Berkeley, no one had asked so directly about my past. I clammed up. It's not that I couldn't answer, it's that I hadn't found the words. I didn't know how to talk about a ruptured heart, a broken life, loss.

I slip into my car, ready for the peace and solitude of my room. I'm not ready to go down the rabbit hole of the past.

Under a hot stream of shower, out of Annice's sphere, the decision to sit for the portrait seems self-effacing and suicidal. Confront my loathed breasts, my wide hips? No, thank you. Now, reconsidering the morning with Annice, I feel inexplicably violated by the inquiry into my family of origin. I'm here to write, not to talk about the past, or last year, or yesterday. Wasn't anonymity one of the payoffs for moving three thousand miles?

Stepping out of the shower, I check the hall to make sure no one is around. I'm wrapped in a thick white towel, organizing my day in my head, brooding over the portrait sitting.

Snap out of it! I have to get on with my day. Bike to Laney for two classes, Spanish and Contemporary Black Literature, and then a two-hour writing session when I return. Maybe I will write about my mother and my sister, the weight of caring for my mother, and how I am going to resolve telling my mother that I am not coming back anytime soon.

* * *

TWO DAYS LATER, I RIDE MY BIKE toward Sacramento Street for the portrait sitting. Annice had apologized for breaching my boundaries. It was fine if I didn't want to share about my past. "Forget about it," she assured. I was appeased. What is impossible to explain to Annice is that I am stuck, my father's death tucked away behind a dam. Not the clean-lined, highly engineered Hoover Dam, but a dam built by a ragtag family of industrious beavers: all twigs, and stems, random branches and leaves. It was messy, it was gnarly, it was flimsy, insubstantial. And it could break at any moment, unleashing a torrent of grief and sadness. Seven years after my father died, I still haven't found the words. My father's death has been swept under the rug, too painful to discuss. No one has given me the words "fragile," "terror," "loss." No one has taught me the words for "loneliness." Whatever I felt at the time of my father's passing was pushed aside in favor of the care of my broken mother. And even if I had the words, I would not own them. The words are shameful. I don't want to be that girl, that child, that person who speaks of empty years, of need, of abandonment.

Winding my way around Berkeley, getting lost sometimes, discovering hidden paths up steep staircases leading to small parks or benches, I am enchanted by this big/small city. One block is a long row of wood-shingled homes, tall trees, almost rustic. The next, urban, the wide swath of green hills omnipresent like a scarf on the neck of weathered, voluptuous beauty.

Pedaling south, I think of Jake. Jake is hot. Her small, hipless body, her mane of curls, her flat chest are the very definition of androgynous. Hers is a boy's body with a halo of curls. With sweet, tender attentions coupled with fierce determination, with lyrical guitar playing and hard-driving drumming, she is both a safe harbor and a dangerous, smoking volcano. I bob happily in the harbor, not wanting to be rained on with steaming ash.

Last week, Jake and I drove up past the golf course to Rock Creek, a beautiful trail that wound through piney woods. Bay laurel and eucalyptus, the air earthy and medicinal. We climbed, breathing hard, to curve around a copse to arrive at Ridge Trail and views of

San Pablo Dam and farther, out toward Contra Costa County. The wide, expansive view placed Berkeley into a larger context. It is one of many cities dotting the wide, rich East Bay with reservoirs and its own volcanic mountain: Mount Diablo. From our high vantage point, we could see the web of BART tracks and, to the east, an endless chain of cookie cutter suburbs.

Now, I pull my bike to the curb to check the address Annice had scribbled: 2237 Curtis. I pedal on past Sacramento Street when the weather changes—the sun is warmer and the temperature spikes. By the time I dismount, I'm sweaty and hot.

"You made it!" Annice whoops, a big smile showing off a row of large but perfectly aligned teeth. She's wearing paint-splattered coveralls and a long-sleeved T-shirt.

We hug amicably.

"For what it's worth," I say, pulling my sweatshirt over my head and untying my shoes.

"It's going to be great," Annice steers us toward the painting studio. "You want a hit?" She lights a joint.

"Nah."

"Tea?"

"Water."

Annice waves me into the studio, a room not unlike my own at Regent Street. Wood panels halfway up the plastered walls, a hardwood floor, leaded glass windows. Outside, bright light embraces camellias, rose bushes, and potato vines.

Annice's friend Dawn is at her easel, sketching a cat perfectly posed in the window frame. "May I?" I peek over her shoulder.

The charcoal sketch reveals the shape of the long-haired calico sitting like an Egyptian statue: a gentle backward C, spiky orange-brown ears and tail curved around its paws like an angora scarf. Looking over her shoulder, I see that Dawn has caught the reflection of the cat in the window, sketching with the lightest hand in silvery charcoal to create a phantom second kitty.

The final arc of the sketcher's hand lifts from the paper. The cat jumps off the windowsill as if on cue, padding toward the kitchen.

Dawn pats my hand. "Okay to pose you on that couch?" she asks, offering up a terrycloth robe still warm from the dryer.

"Fine," I answer feeling as somber as if I'm going to my own funeral.

Heading into the bathroom to undress, my body cools. 1950s pink wall tiles and black and white floor are a short refuge. Off with the fleece, the T-shirt, the jeans. Off with the bra, the panties, the socks. In my mind's eye I can see Dawn sketching the phantom kitty and realize how poets employ a similar way of seeing: work lightly to capture the physical and its reflection, the obvious and the not so obvious. The rendering and the imagining, the real and the make-believe, the seed of an idea and a fully blossomed poem.

I slip into the thick, warm robe.

On the velvet couch, Annice arranges my body to catch the light, focusing on the slant of sun flooding the window where the cat had just dozed. One hand on my head, one on the small of my back, she arranges my long hair to drape over the couch arm. Torso toward the room and the artists' easels, she retrieves a large, felted hat to perch on my head.

"Rakish," Annice laughs her throaty laugh. "It's you. Mysterious and rakish." She belts out another hearty laugh. "Great. Don't move."

I relax into the soft cushions when I realize that my pubis is on full display. In a moment of anxiety, I reach for the robe. Annice waves it away. "Nothing special," she says. "I've seen more than one." With a last adjustment to bend the right leg over the left, Annice gives the thumbs up.

"Thirty, forty minutes?" Dawn asks.

"Sure." I blanch at Dawn's request. I don't think I've sat in one position for thirty minutes since the sixth grade.

Sensing my dismay, Dawn says, by way of consolation, "We can break, stretch, have tea."

"Fine," I offer, steeling myself.

"And go for another thirty?" Dawn asks.

If I don't start writhing, talking to myself, or singing the song that's stuck in my head since last Tuesday, I think.

Annice is already hard at work, her hands flying around her palette like a windmill.

I settle in, willing my mind to slow, my body to still. I close my eyes, hoping that the internal landscape offers a hiding place from two pairs of penetrating eyes. For amusement, I plan the rest of my day: bike home, at least one hour at my desk, shop for dinner. Tonight I'm going to see *The Paper Chase* with Nancy.

Before I can start daydreaming about new poems, movies, and friends, a picture of the woman I met last week at the White Horse flashes across my mind: Sonya.

"Come see me. My booth is between Channing and Durant," she invited when I complimented her earrings.

I hadn't visited yet. Maybe this week.

I'm wondering what it will be like to see her at her place of work after our passionate kiss. A poem starts to form, out of the blue.

Little kitty/content on your sill/do you know you are an object of a painter's scrutiny, a portrait sitter, a lark?

Now. What rhymes with lark? The next line takes me by surprise.

Little kitty/content on your sill, are you content, or lonely for a friend?

How will I remember the lines? I can't stop the session to ask for a pen and paper, but poems evaporate. I try to hold the two short lines in my mind, thinking of words to rhyme with sill and scrutiny.

"Break!" Annice stands up from her easel. I reach for the robe on the arm of the sofa, stepping across the room for my bag with a pad and pen. Poem scribbled, I lean over to inspect Annice's canvas.

"No peeking," she covers the canvas with a silk cloth. Across the room, Dawn follows suit.

"How was posing?" Dawn asks, stretching down to her toes.

"Better and worse than expected," I say, stretching my back.

"I told you it wasn't so bad," Annice chimes in. "You were great. I like what I'm getting," Annice congratulates me. "Great curves, great lines. I love your strong legs, especially your calves," she bends down to stroke my bare legs. "I'm being kind to your breasts," she says, gently ribbing me.

"Minimizing? I'll love you forever!"

"Poetic license," Dawn interjects.

We muse on artistic license. "As long as you are not making me square-headed like Picasso," I tease.

CHAPTER **6**

Jewish in the Diaspora

December. By the middle of the month, the frosty mornings and a rare cold snap have loosened their grip. Two sunny days have warmed the house, the lashing winter rains a gray memory. I'm down from three layers to two: flannel pajamas, sweatshirt. Over a breakfast of bland oatmeal and carrot juice, I indulge in a muscular Assam tea.

I need to find a place to write. "In Budapest," Cloud bemoans, "many cafés designated special tables for writers. A separate menu too, with rock bottom prices: a hearty soup, a hunk of bread, and, of course, coffee and a simple pastry." Her description of the Hungarian institution is so seductive that I can't stop hoping to discover one in Berkeley. Why not? Berkeley has imported the European coffee house, the New York jazz club, the theater. I envy a culture that so respects its writers it created a safe space to ensure sufficient nourishment to think big thoughts. Poor America, worshipping only the dollar. Granted, there is the academic route of fellowships and funding for emerging writers and artists, but, absent a benefactor, we are left to fend for ourselves. While financial challenges have created a few creative solutions—warehouses converted to studios like Project Artaud in San Francisco and the old fish-packing district in the Berkeley flats; communes, houseboats, and other varieties of cheap housing—it isn't the same as striding down to the local café to sit, uninterrupted. With ingenuity, a little penury, and patience (which bakeries were tossing out leftovers at 8:00 p.m.? Which restaurants disposing of edible produce?), an artist could afford a room of her own. Still, it isn't the same as knowing that the local café has your back, or your soup bowl, as it were. Soon, I'll be able to write in the school library. For now, I remain on the prowl for the perfect, quiet spot.

Cloud's travels, a half a year bumming around Europe with a girlfriend and a backpack to Spain, France, Italy, Greece, and Turkey, was her "post doc" after her graduation from the University of Michigan. The minute I escaped high school I had no interest in bumming around. I was hell-bent on getting on track as an activist and writer. As romantic as sleeping in abandoned lofts, barns and warehouses, hostels and beaches, rooftops and homestays sounds, it pales in comparison to my Berkeley life. Someday, I will bum around. But now is a moment, and I am smack in the center of it. Cloud aspires to write, but her energy, as challenging to harness as a bucking bronco, won't allow her to sit still for more than an hour at a time. Her plans are mercurial; one day she wants to be a writer, the next a visual artist, the next, she is applying to an ashram, and when she tires, she researches osteopathic colleges.

I find the Café Renaissance on Bancroft. Mornings are best there for catching the writing wave, with warm sun pouring in from its two-story windows. With students in classes, the café is blissfully uncrowded. I might not have a special writer's menu, but if I buy a cappuccino and a croissant I can settle in for an hour or two without being shot the hairy eyeball from a go-getter wiping my table for the fourteenth time.

I grab the *Chronicle* from the front porch, slipping the rubber band off the blue plastic wrapping and adding it to the detritus already threatening to overflow the kitchen junk drawer.

"Equal Rights Amendment (ERA) Contested in Debate at Mills College: Dunlap vs. Schlafly." I read the article in depth but am challenged to make sense of it. Phyllis Schlafly, a conservative from Florida, is contesting ratification of the ERA because, if passed, Schlafly contests women will not be exempt from military service and will lose the "right to be supported by our husbands." I am indignant; beside the fact that I don't believe our military would actively recruit women via the ERA, equal pay, childcare, and the end of job discrimination are a small price to pay for that risk. The problem is that Schlafly is gaining ground. Though Berkeley is its own social and political bubble—its foundation built on co-ops, public radio, art, education, and a healthy way of life—we are still subject to federal and state laws.

Communities of theosophists, health food enthusiasts, homeopaths, naturopaths, Buddhists, and union organizers have thrived for decades. Not to mention that the University of California (UC) system was formed to create a democratic network of higher education that is open to everyone who qualifies. The UC system is the west's answer to the Ivy League, minus the quotas, social stratification, and snobbery.

Is it something in the water here?

Regardless of the permissive atmosphere, I have my worries: higher education might be democratic, but that doesn't answer the question of how I will earn a living as a poet.

And now, the drum beat of separatism is beginning to pound. Women-only concerts, cafés, conferences, softball teams, and readings are growing in popularity. Men are not welcome. Am I ready for a life without men? It seems that the longer I hang around, the price of admission is to commit a sin of omission, to swear off my ties to men and all systems, beliefs, and practices stemming from a male-dominated society.

Teacup in the sink, I throw on jeans and a sweatshirt and grab my scratched-up Peugeot out of our sad, shabbily furnished living room. Secondhand chairs that explode with stuffing are covered in Indian saris, sheets hang on the windows and random fabric from Value Village. The living room is a waystation and storage room for amps, bikes, books, and instruments. I lock the door behind me and start up the hill.

* * *

THE DAYS AFTER THE RAIN always shine brighter, the sky clearer, the gardens grown greener overnight. I pedal hard across Grove Street and up Russell, the incline minor but demanding. Past the sweet, well-kept bungalows, past the house where Malvina Reynolds (the composer of the song "Little Boxes") lives, a mural of poppies painted on the side. Past the car dealers on Shattuck Avenue, and finally to Telegraph. At the corner of the Park and Shop, I turn left and pedal north to the four-block stretch where vendors have license to display everything from handmade baby clothes to knitted sweaters, Fillmore East posters, photographs of rock bands, hand-turned pottery, wooden bowls, and beaded jewelry. Joy inches its way back, my heart and mind easing out of frustration about Schlafly and the ERA and back into the moment. It's early December—not officially winter—but as warm as a September day in New York City. I'm in a sweatshirt and jeans. It may have been cold and damp last week, but an east coast winter this certainly is not.

Shriveled brown sycamore leaves scrape across the sidewalks, the brittle sound reminding me of another bright, late fall day in

Brooklyn. In slow motion, the memory comes into focus like a photograph in a chemical bath.

I reach for my father's hand. In his other, he holds his tallis bag, a deep midnight blue velvet bag with silver lettering that I don't understand but feel its magic.

We are walking to synagogue on a Saturday morning. Rosh Hashanah and Yom Kippur are over, and for the first time I am allowed into the cavernous sanctuary. A cantor sings soulfully in a sonorous voice. The holidays are a strange time in our house; all goes quiet. My father disappears to services, buys his tickets, and goes on his own to pray.

"Sukkot," my father explains as I look up at his tall frame, "used to be one of the most important Jewish holidays."

"More than Passover and Yom Kippur?" I ask.

"Not more…" he continues. "The first harvest was designated as a celebration. The people danced and ate together in 'sukkahs,' or little temporary booths in the field."

I don't care what day or holiday it is, I'm alone with my father, secure and safe in his large presence. The pews are sparsely populated, but when the Rabbi pulls a tallis over his head, the prayer I hear supercharges my spirit and changes my life.

Shma yisrael. Adonai eloheinu. Adonai echad.

Passionate voices converge in more than prayer, more than recitation. In a communal crying, each to their own call of yearning, I hear a call that shakes me to my core. Their prayer is not a yearning for food, or shelter, or even for companionship, but for something bigger, ineffable: a yearning for God. The hair on my head shivers with electricity, as if I've stuck my finger into a hot, live electrical socket. I close my eyes. The tallis is removed from congregants' heads, the frisson passes….

Now, riding my Peugeot in the sunshine on a December morning, questions tug at me like a dog on its chain: Is it time to pick up the threads of my Jewish life? Hannukah is coming. Am I going to ignore it? And what of Passover? These rituals once defined my year, but then again, they revolved around family. Aunts and uncles, cousins and grandparents gathered to mark the sacred occasions and enjoy Grandma's brisket and relax. It was the cycle of the year with which I had been branded: High Holidays, Hannukah, Passover. Repeat.

At Telegraph and Dwight Way, I hop off the bike, hoping that the redwood menorah I saw a week ago is still there. Avenue craftspeople come and go like the breeze.

Colorful flyers catch my eye with a wild variety of fonts, advertising poetry readings at iconic bookstores—Cody's: Julia Vinograd, Diane di Prima; Moe's: Gregory Corso and Michael McClure. Concert flyers, on heavier stock and more artfully produced, are wrapped around utility poles, thumbtacked to bulletin boards, and posted in store windows. I get out my notepad and jot down dates for "Commander Cody and His Lost Planet Airmen," "J. Geils," and "Dan Hicks and His Hot Licks." I already have tickets for a Grateful Dead show at the Fillmore; Jake, Tzippah, Michael, Arthur, and I are going to drive to the Fillmore East for the New Year's Eve show.

The sun climbs. I stop, ripping off my sweatshirt. High noon rings from the Campanile. The sound of the gargantuan bells imbues the city with an ethereal magic, a deep brass ringing from the tower's height is music raining down as drops of dew.

This street, this artery that stretches from downtown Oakland straight into the beating heart of campus, is where Berkeley life vibrates. Here on the Ave is the festivity of street vendors, invitations to hear, to listen, to explore, to grow. Bookstores for the mind, cafés for the buzz and conversation with friends and strangers, foods from the world over remind us that while we are living in the United

States, we are citizens of the world. Here, in this northeast corner of the Bay Area, in a small town in the center of a gigantic state, is asylum, is refuge, is safety.

Crossing Channing Way and past John's Soup Kitchen, an early lunch crowd spoons soup and munches on hearty brown bread. I pass a street parade of book sellers and buyers churning through Shakespeare's (secondhand books), Shambala (dedicated to all things spiritual), and Moe's, where the cigar-smoking purveyor of good new and used books welcomes all to the basement for poetry readings. Finally, Cody's, the high church of all things literary and the site of the best flower stand in town.

The Ave is ground zero not only for poetry but for everything from tiny cups of espresso to the Goddess Kali, Yogananda, Meher Baba, Richard Alpert, Gurumayi, Hari Krishna. It is ground zero from the flower seller to the European bakery (with its Linzer torte, croissants, and brioche) to the herb store selling loose herbs, teas, supplements, and oils to concoct recipes for healing.

Protesters stand on streetcorners, placards demand that UC divest in South Africa, street preachers call for the return of Jesus, and dark men in keffiyehs shout "Israel out of Palestine," while a longhair on a soapbox exhorts all to read Mao's "Little Red Book," a bible of proletariat dialectic.

Last year, I was on Fifth Avenue on a hot summer day in New York City, hurrying to a summer job in the baby department of a mid-level department store. The city assaulted my senses, my spirit, and was swallowing me whole. Loud, booming construction sites, broken subways, men groping, masturbating in cars, muggings, murders were daily, unsavory fare. In Berkeley, life is the polar opposite for me: we are out of doors in the fresh, clean air, we go out at night on our bicycles, with our cars, our lives are wide and broad. In Berkeley, even creative acts are political: poetry is political, our bodies are political.

What we eat? Political. If I can change someone's mind with a poem, if I can help them to feel seen, my work is worth the time.

At Café Mediterranean, Julia Vinograd (the poet we call "the bubble lady" for the bubbles she blows as she parades up and down Telegraph) discusses the scene at People's Park with a clutch of poets. Dressed as a renaissance bard in a velvet hat of gold and brown, a long skirt, and velvet shirt, Julia limps down the street, a UC Berkeley and University of Iowa dropout.

Nearing Haste, I survey the vendors. A small place inside me hopes to see Rick, the copper-haired jeweler with the long ponytail, but first, I spy the menorah hidden among the wooden Christmas tree ornaments, hand-turned bowls, and bread boards crafted from redwood.

The artisan smiles sweetly. The connection I usually have with Jewish people (a knowing glance, a referential schmooze about the holiday) is missing. I wonder why this blond-haired, blue-eyed Californian is hawking Jewish items but decide not to ask.

Slipping the package into my backpack, I walk my bike two blocks to Sonya's booth.

"Hey you," she sings. Sonya twists wire and beads into delicate, shiny creations that look part spider web, part sculpture. "Wearable art," she gracefully informs, patting a nylon folding chair.

"I love hanging out on the Ave," Sonya starts, "mixing it up with people, selling my wares."

"Flirting," I tease.

"Yes, flirting. Part of the job."

Sonya is the first woman entrepreneur I've met. I'm enthralled. With a sudden burst, students rush small storefronts for lunch. Falafels, burritos, burgers, pizza slices—as long as it can be held in one hand. Two tall, young, athletic-looking women stop to examine Sonya's wares. Julia Vinograd limps by, smiling and blowing bubbles.

The Ave is her life. Books of her poems are stashed in her newsboy's canvas bag. Today I stop her, buy a copy. I open to a poem, mid-book:

LISTENING TO THE RADIO
I am listening to the radio.
I am not listening to the radio.
I am listening to the silence in my room
behind the radio.
I am the radio. Listen.

As Sonya chats up the undergrads, I am inspired by Vinograd's spareness, the paradox between being and not being, silence and presence. I scribble notes for a poem about my hike yesterday in Strawberry Canyon.

I'm packing up to head off to write when Sonya grabs me and kisses me right there on Telegraph Avenue. Her lips are sweet, tasting of mango and citrus tea. I kiss her right back.

"Is this legal?" I whisper.

"Duh! Of course it is!"

"Whew! Catch you later. I'll make you dinner," I offer.

We squeeze each other affectionately. The closeness of Sonya's soft body is comforting and familiar.

"Come with me to Suze's," I invite her to the party on Sunday. "There will be latkes."

Sonya smiles. I've been elusive, buzzing in and out of her life, not always around when she wants me. I don't feel guilty, I just want to keep her interested.

"I'll check my schedule," she winks, turning back to close an earring deal with the two women.

Sauntering off, I wonder how the two undergrads enjoyed our public display of affection. Sonya finds my Jewish practice charming; she identifies as "culturally Jewish" only. But maybe she didn't have her hair stand up like mine, or have a father who took her to *shul*. My Jewish life is my connection to the best thing about my attenuated childhood: my father.

Settled on my bike, I sling the backpack on, the menorah snuggled up with my legal pads, Julia Vinograd's book, and pens.

The day warms to shirtsleeves weather. I grab a coffee and set up near the creek on campus. It's not a table in Budapest, but it is serviceable enough: a picnic bench in a sunny spot near a circle of redwood trees. Riding the rest of the way down Telegraph, I wait at the light at Bancroft Avenue, words for two new poems colliding in my head.

CHAPTER 7

The Band

Ready for a change, Nancy Henderson finds a new band. Five women join together as if by a greater hand, gathered up by divine artistic power. What Jake, Debbie, Suzanne, and Nancy Vogl lack in formal musical training, Nancy Henderson competently covers. Because both are named Nancy, Nancy Vogl has been nick-named "Vogie" and Nancy Henderson "Hendo."

Hendo, a Julliard dropout, is a natural composer. The perfect chord choices and harmonies are her specialty. Vogie (a self-taught guitarist, saxophonist, banjo player, singer, and songwriter) is the master of gentle, lyrical runs on her Guild D-40. Vogie has the voice of a husky bird and the looks of a surfer. Jake is a musician in the vein of John Lennon, blessed with native talent, musical intuition, and an innate sense of rhythm. Debbie is the band's Dylan-esque poet who has learned enough chords to strum a proper tune to accompany her fighting words. Debbie's reputation is widespread in Portland, where her powerful lyrics and hard strumming guitar have turned into a clarion call for the dykes of the great Northwest. Suzanne plays bass, adding cool licks, and her own repertoire of songs.

The timing couldn't have been better for them to form the Berkeley Women's Music Collective: Jake was tired of being the "girl" drummer in a long string of male-led bands, Hendo was ready to break away from the Red Star Singers and call something her own, and Debbie had been searching for a band the way that Patti Smith did—music exalted her words and gave her people to play with, musically and otherwise. With a simple handwritten sign posted at the Berkeley Co-Op, Debbie Lempke created the band of her dreams. And the chemistry was right. Each member brought a unique set of skills and musical knowledge to make the whole larger than the sum of its parts.

In April of 1973, the first National Gathering of Lesbians is held on the UCLA campus, organized by the activist Jeanne Cordova. At open mic on the last day, Vogie, Debbie Lempke, and Woody Simmons discover one other. A few months later, responding to the sign at the Co-Op, Jake and Hendo are brought on. The band stages their first outdoor gig: a debut in People's Park, which is to be a benefit concert for the SLA's food giveaway.

The band is invited to headline at the Santa Cruz Women's Music Festival along with Meg Christian, Cris Williamson, Holly Near, and Baba Yaga. High in the redwoods, a stage is built. Rock and roll performed by an all-lesbian band in the shade of the trees is about as perfect a moment as I could have ever dreamed.

The audience is fired up; there's enough energy to power a substation. We are a collection of women in transition, most of us with an inchoate understanding of the cruelty that could be unleashed toward us. There are women who left husbands and children to join the swelling ranks of women bent on change and self-realization. There are women who have been sequestered in small towns, unable to find their tribe. There are artists who haven't been given a chance in the male-dominated worlds of film, sculpture, and painting. There are victims: victims of abuse, sexism, racism, and genderism. We are women who have been closeted, facing lives of solitude and despair. But here we are—together. Black, White, Asian, Pagan, Jewish, Baptist. We couldn't believe our good luck. It's nirvana, it's magical, it unleashes possibility. The bands play, we dance, and we raise the energy in that redwood grove to make change.

Some nights after, a spontaneous jam session erupts at a Derby Street house party. Vogie casually strums her rhythm guitar, Jake picks up an acoustic twelve-string, Hendo settles at the piano. A tall, sturdy-looking Black woman named Ajida sits in on congas. Debbie skips the party to visit friends in town from Portland.

Bonnie Lockhart, Hendo's old bandmate from the locally famous Red Star Singers, jumps in instead. The jam was a cross between upbeat folk and low-key rock, a space that had been dominated by the Joy of Cooking, Crosby, Stills & Nash, and others. It is fast becoming a unique, California sound: intense but laid back, musically complex while packing a bold political message, compelling, but not danceable.

The band knows well that it is standing on the shoulders of Laura Nyro, Carole King, and Carly Simon: the magnificent soloists who broke through the male-dominated rock music scene. But a woman's band is a different animal. A woman's band is not five women hired for backup, not sidekicks to the men, but front and center. There is something magnificent about a group of women belting out Suzanne's "Fury," cranking up the volume, demanding to be heard. I left that party convinced that we were an army of joyful warriors!

I am content to be the band's Fan Club President and mascot. Why wouldn't I be? Their artistry is like a mandala, the lines of connection and talent interweave and complement while they inspire and challenge each other. There is the sweet, there is the sour, there is the hard-hitting and the soft touch. Moods and songs are many, and the fans eat it up, all of it. I am part of a collaboration that will change musical history, provide a soundtrack for the women's movement forming, and bring joy to legions of women who are dedicating themselves to fighting the good fight.

CHAPTER 8

Falling-Down House

Jake and I get the opportunity to make a new home together, and Debbie decides to join us. As luck would have it, friends of our roommate Tam are vacating their falling-down house in South Berkeley. I load my meager possessions into milk crates and fill my sturdy rucksack, stuffing it all into Cherry Bomb. Just two miles from the tree-lined campus neighborhood, I settle into the grit of South Berkeley. The falling-down house is ugly, it is decrepit, but we each have a room and it is our own place. No random wanderers, a clean kitchen and a door that locks.

I trade the redwood tree and Cecile Brunners outside my window at 2619 Regent Street for a view of a scrappy backyard and some rustling cottonwoods. So, soon after Jake, Debbie, and I moved in, I rent a rototiller, fighting to break up the hard clay soil native to the Berkeley flats. After adding soil amendments, turning it over again, and letting it rest for a week, I plant and transform the ugly dirt yard into an abundant patch of living earth. Sunflowers, lettuce, broccoli, zucchinis, and eggplants nestled in, waiting for spring. Now, the much-needed rain beats out a steady rhythm. Fat raindrops cling to leafless branches in the newly cultivated garden just outside my bedroom window. The rain, the only actual weather in Berkeley besides summer fog, pulls the world in a little closer.

I am glad for the inert day. When the sun is up, warming the falling-down house, the call to run or bike, hike, or even sit on the front porch, distracts and compels as strongly as the Sirens who called Odysseus. The sun is a seducer, but I am training myself to resist, if just a little, to stay inside and write.

Debbie, Jake, and I have spent the morning drinking coffee, eating boiled eggs over rice, and planning our calendars so each of us can enjoy some alone time in the falling-down house.

"Tuesdays are Joan's day, Wednesday Jake's. Thursday is Debbie's." We sketch out the month on a fresh legal pad.

"Except when there's a gig, right?" Debbie asks.

As the newest member of the group, Debbie tends to defer to Jake or me on house decisions. Conciliatory. That's what she's been. Go with the flow. The band is another story. There, she is an equal member, weighing in on everything from set lists to splitting the take, from how far the band would travel to how much should be contributed to the band fund.

I'm not concerned about missing a night alone because of a gig. The question is: what will I do on my exiled nights? Poetry readings, movies, visits with friends are all well and good, but my hope is that the alone time will be fruitful for writing. But where? Cafés are fine during the day, but the cacophony of espresso machines, music, and conversation is too distracting in the evenings. I can possibly get a visitor's pass to one of the libraries on the UC Berkeley campus, but I wouldn't know how to begin to crack the code that is the staunch university's permission system.

Falling-Down House

After our house meeting, Jake washes the dishes then takes off to see Lynn. Although she is seeing Debbie—who is in love with her—Jake is slippery: she is in love with Lynn. Lynn had left her husband, Ken—the father of her beautiful child, Vanessa—for Jake. Ken is enraged at being replaced by Jake…a woman! It gets ugly. Women don't leave Ken, and he doesn't buy that Lynn is a lesbian. And he certainly can't abide that not only has his wife left him, but left him for a woman. He pours sugar into Jake's gas tank, he makes idle threats, he is apoplectic.

Today, Jake tells me, she and Lynn can finally have some alone time. Debbie drives to Derby Street for band practice. Usually, the quiet, empty house is inspiration enough, but lately, I've been struggling when it comes time to sit at my desk. I have resorted to tricks: setting a timer for an hour, or starting by revising a poem to get the creative juices flowing. Now that the first rush of "being a poet" is receding, I find that the job isn't a simple recipe of inspiration and typing my poems, that time and work, focus and revisions are as important a part of the process as capturing the initial spark, that first fragment. I am, if hesitatingly, accepting the many levels of work required to become a real writer: the multiple drafts, the critique groups, open mics and early readers, struggling over lines, and the frustration when the right words refuse to materialize.

Clean and dirty clothes litter the floor, books are scattered everywhere. Teacups, a crusty bowl from yesterday's oatmeal clutter, candles, pens, paper, and textbooks cover every flat surface. Gathering dirty clothes into a laundry bag, my mind gnaws on that developing wrinkle in the community that has got me on edge: men versus women. At every turn, women pose opinions, lobby for their positions: we should eschew the company of men, embrace separatism. Men are our oppressors, enemies to be banished.

Dirty clothes in the laundry bag and clean ones returned to drawers, dirty dishes soaking in the kitchen sink, the bed made, and the floor swept, I can fabricate no further distraction. I grab a pad and pen: men are not my enemy. Men are in residence, deep in my heart. My father, friends, uncles, cousins. Banish men? Why? I'm not buying it for myself, but I'm anxious because I sense Debbie and Jake have begun to lean into the divisive stance.

Above my desk, an enlarged photograph of Annice's portrait hangs. I was appalled when Annice presented it to me. I didn't recognize even a modicum of likeness, in the heavy strokes of browns and yellows, in my faraway look. There was no spark of joy or the smile that, to me, was a defining feature. What I did see was the narrow eyes, the furrowed brow, the large breasts.

"I've entered the portrait into a group show," Annice told me. "I hope you're okay with the photograph for now."

"The photograph is fine as long as you don't require my presence if the painting is accepted," I say, horrified at the prospect of onlookers comparing me to the painting.

My face in this painting is not the face I see in the mirror. The lines are different. The skin tone is different. Even the emotions telegraphed in the painting are different. In the mirror I see sharp outlines of cheek bones. I see bright eyes and flat, unexpressive lips. Annice chose a side-facing angle that obscured the cheeks and only minorly involved the eyes. I just don't see what she sees, and in fact, I see myself in the mirror as more friendly, more open than her portrait. Aren't portraits supposed to flatter? And yet, Annice is thrilled with her outcome, pronounced it a success! She thinks I look "mysterious" and "glamorous." She believes that she has captured a movie-star likeness. Her painting partner, Dawn, never got past a charcoal sketch, a sketch I like much more! Her delicate lines and the light touch of her pencil have, in their subtlety, captured more of my essence; I can sense wonder in that contemplative view, even a hint of delight. In Annice's version I appear brooding to the point of morose. And although that is a side of me, it isn't a side I necessarily want on public display.

I forget about writing, at least for the moment. I love the falling-down house when it is quiet. The rain eases, but I can still hear soft pattering on the roof, like the slow drip of coffee through a filter, an auger of good things to come. The rain feeds my plants, the plants will feed us. Being closer to the earth and to nature has calmed me— living closer to the ground, a safe foundation.

The past few months, I've been studying photography, jazz improvisation, and Chinese philosophers at Laney. Oh, and also Spanish conversation and French new wave cinema. After the slog of high school, the tedious requirements, the perennial tests, finally attending college, where I am encouraged to honor and explore my passions, has reignited my love of learning.

The only one of our crowd still in school, I secretly relish the balance of school's schedules, structure and discipline of homework with my renegade life. I've always been a good student, but the idea of leaving high school straight for college seemed like going from one prison to another. A whole world is out here! Who wants to be sequestered away on a college campus? Berkeley is the best of both worlds: intellectually stimulating while allowing me the freedom to live in the adult world.

While photography is the most serious contender for my attention, writing has won my heart. Still, I will pursue photography alongside my writing classes, at least for a while. The camera informs the writing in every image; scrutinizing the physical world helps me to home in on details I may have missed had I not been drawn to photograph them as subjects: a statue of Pan playing the flute in a neighbor's secret garden, a child holding a sign at a protest on the steps at Sproul Plaza, the Navarro river's mirrored reflection, Jake in a calm mood, tall sunflowers and zucchini blossoms in my garden, golden light on the beach at sunset.

But lately I've discovered that even close looking does not necessarily mean that I will be successful in capturing what I see. "The human eye is the perfect camera," my friend Joan tells me when I complain about a picture not developing the way that I had seen it. Writing has posed similar frustrations; the thoughts don't always travel through the pen, just as Annice's hand, in my opinion, didn't nail my image in paint. In photography class at Laney, we learn about aperture openings, capturing varying qualities of light, and how changing up the combinations of chemicals could affect an image in the darkroom. The artist's challenge: to replicate, or to embellish?

"I am listening to the radio. I am not listening to the radio." Julia Vinograd's line of verse is stuck in my craw. In the end, art is a blank canvas on which the observer projects their own perspective, history, and world view. My job is to render, to open, to inspire, whether it is with exactitude or with an unexpected flourish. My job is to be more like Annice's studio partner, Dawn, deftly but lightly suggesting an image.

I turn back to my still-blank legal pad. I want to give up and I want to express my discomfort with the emerging separatist demand to banish men. The separatists argue that by eliminating men the spotlight will shine only on us. I think of the male-dominated poetry scene I gingerly investigated just before I left New York. Inspiring but intimidating. The church on Second Avenue teemed with successful, ambitious poets: John Berryman, John Ashbery, Kenneth Rexroth, Allen Ginsberg. A few women were allowed entry into the club: Anne Waldman, Ruth Weiss, Patti Smith. I was young, and unformed. They were on track; I was still trying to catch the train.

The rain stops. I jiggle the window in its rotten frame, securing a sturdy book to hold it up. The ropes on this double hung frayed long ago.

I consider the trope of life without men: as irritating as a splinter, too small to remove, too big to ignore.

Here, in our little feminist bubble, the community we have created absent of men, I've been given a chance. I've been seen! I am grateful, I am awed, I am moved by the warm inclusion of the women's artistic community, despite being younger than most by several years. I've never felt so welcome, so…a-piece-of. The insular world we have worked hard to create has benefits. (We are empowered! We are honored! We are valued!)

At the same time, I see that women can also be the purveyors of hurt, a hurt that diminishes their lovers, damages self-esteem, and causes harm.

Yes, I see how men dominate conversations, business, the film industry, publishing, and academia. I see doors open to men that aren't open to us. Yes, I need distance from men to create without male judgement. But ditching all men for the cause of feminist advancement? It doesn't sit right. I am not sure I am ready to live in a world without them.

I decide to allow myself free rein. No rules, no limits. I will sleep with whom I want, when I want and where I want. I will fraternize with my male friends and keep my father's memory alive. I will find peace in the liminal space, even if it means being alone in my position.

But I am not ready to write about it. I am not prepared to risk offending, confronting, or engaging in philosophical disagreements. I am not ready to stand out, to be the one to say: Are we sure these rules aren't as oppressive as the rules set by men? Are we sure that "going against" is in fact more effective than cooperation? And, I am not ready to get loud.

I put the worrisome thoughts aside, stop fretting about whether my image in the portrait is true, file my anxiety away. Poetry is elusive, not to be caught in my net today. I let it go, confident that I will catch it soon.

I'll go out, I think. Maybe poetry is outside today in the rain-stained tree branches, in the soaked gardens, in a painting in a museum or in the sound of the wind howling down a canyon.

The rain starts up again and a drip-drop alerts me to a leak sprung over the window frame facing west, toward the garden. In the kitchen I dig out a plastic bucket. Our falling-down house is porous, it is drafty, it is ugly, but it is also a badge of honor that allows us freedom from financial stress. The one-hundred-dollar rent gifts us time and space.

"Send some spray my way/I'm feeling lonely..."

With that, the poetry butterfly flits away. I slip on a warm rain jacket and rev up Cherry Bomb.

CHAPTER 9

Green Tara: Goddess of Liberation

In the *zendo*, a flyer announces an exhibit of Tibetan *thangkas*. In a light drizzle, I head up Parker Street to Grove Street, a usually busy thoroughfare, quiet on this gray Sunday afternoon. Nestled in a grove, sculptural arms of black oaks are locked in an embrace with the small Live Oak art gallery. Inside, a redwood paneled room explodes in a riot of color.

Meandering trance-like around the perimeter of the gallery, I am drawn as if by magnets to the thousand Bodhisattvas. Rainbows, lotus flowers, blue sky, blue rivers, and white puffy clouds are meticulous, the monks who create the *thangkas* trained in patience with miniscule brushes and painstaking rendering. The *thangkas* are framed in layers of rich, embroidered silk. Ordinarily covered, the *thangkas* remain behind a silk curtain when not employed for meditation. Now, with twenty or more on full view, a sacred vibration permeates the room, the silence deep and rich. I take in the many gates of enlightenment that gods and goddesses must pass through—reincarnations, lifetimes, turns of the karmic wheel.

Midway around the gallery I am caught short. Gazing upon Green Tara (a woman!), Bodhisattva of compassion, I have a dizzying sense of looking at myself. Bulbous breasts, voluptuous, luscious melons (as my sister ridiculed) are on full, self-loving display. No shame in the female. Tara, rooted, grounded, is posed in a yogic tree pose with bells on her ankles and a small cloth covering her pudendum. Her hands are in Anjali Mudra, bestowing kindness, love, and healing. Alone in the gallery, I slip off my rain jacket and sit on the hardwood floor directly in front of the *tangka*.

Meditating on the resplendent female image, the peaceful gaze of equanimity on her round face, the shapeliness of her legs and arms, I sense a message: ground in yourself, always inhabit your body, and you will be a sight to gaze upon and a source of healing. Sitting in front of the *tangka*, calming my mind, I ponder my sense of kinship with Tara.

What I learn is that Tara is not revered for having "done" anything in the Western sense, but for the blessing of her own empowerment. Tara utilizes her power only for good, for healing and emanating compassion. The image of Tara lights up a dark place of doubt and confusion that has plagued me this past year. I've been struggling with paradigms, philosophies, and manifestos, some of which resonate and some of which frighten me. Smash the patriarchy with incendiary verbiage, actions, and protests, or be a peaceful force for good? Feed people or employ violence as some of the more radical factions have embraced? The Black Panthers started to simply feed children, but came to the conclusion that the only way to change the situation of African Americans in a meaningful way is violence; the People's Liberation Front and the SLA, employing military tactics to make their points, have become targets for the FBI. Arrests result in ruined lives, and in some cases, death. I am balancing in two worlds, wanting change and spiritual development—but at what cost?

Buddhist teaching eschews the dichotomy of "good versus evil," rather embracing learning to recognize and own our "negativity" and all that is destructive. It teaches that destruction is part of life, that beings have been reincarnated multiple times before arriving at nirvana. Tara is the embodiment of a prayer, a bright light, a powerful healer. Is a true Berkeley Revolution a destruction of the negative forces within us, or the negative forces outside? Is Mao's Cultural Revolution really a force in China and the world as many factions here in Berkeley espouse? Is banishing intellects and artists to "re-pro-gramming" camps really productive, or does it simply perpetuate the cycle of violence? Is art truly a bourgeoise pursuit? Are learning and study to be relegated to the dustbin of history?

I leave the museum vibrating. Outside, I enjoy a cool mist. I am grateful for the gray sky that dampens my racing mind. Gods, goddesses, bodhisattvas, angels, rainbows, enlightenment. The show was a bright window, a visit to a sacred Himalayan temple, a moun-tain monastery, an enlightened church.

I drive back in the crepuscular light to the falling-down house in a state of wonderment. Galleries and museums have always been doors to inspiration, and this afternoon is going into the hall of fame. During the last years of high school, with seniors on a split schedule and school released at 2:00 p.m., I took to venturing into Manhattan alone. There, I wandered the MOMA. Each department offered new possibilities; each gallery opened new worlds.

I was changed in those galleries as art provided a respite from my world of pain. Paintings, color, shapes, and the effusive joy in those works held me, if just briefly, in beauty, erasing the grief of our little apartment. Kandinsky and Miro spoke to the lightness of spirit and joy inside of me that had not found expression. A lust for life flooded the frames in bright colors and quirky shapes. I hadn't learned yet that Kandinsky had studied synesthesia, the correlation of color to sound and by extension, to the emotions. Color theory, art theory, cubism, fauvism, impressionism, modernism—the academics had no bearing on the joy the paintings evoked.

At the MOMA, Monet's room-sized triptych of water lilies and Picasso's *Guernica* were on display, teaching me that an artist could claim huge spaces, could demand it. Live large! I returned time and again, roaming galleries a private joy I didn't want to share. In solitude, I could linger, the neurons of my brain set on fire. The Museum of Modern Art was my schoolroom, my university, my mentor, and my friend.

When I arrive home, still trembling with the intensity of the *thangkas*, a fluffy grey kitten is curled in a ball on the doorstep. No collar, no identification. I name her Tara.

That night, the day of art and *thangkas* receding, I lie in bed, petting Tara and wondering when I am going to call my mother. Last night over dinner I asked Jake if she would keep me company while I broke the news that I was a lesbian and that I wouldn't be coming home anytime soon.

CHAPTER 10

Latkes at Suze's

Latkes at Suze's are to Hannukah what twinkly lights outlining
roofs are to Christmas, not absolutely necessary, but a warm addi-
tion to winter holidays. Susie and Nevin's house is filled to capacity
with every Jewish lesbian in Berkeley.

"Hanging from the rafters," Sonya will quip later when we leave at
the fuck-everything hour of 1:00 a.m. on a Sunday night.

While the latkes are tasty and appropriately greasy (prepared in
advance by Suze so she would have ample time to work the room),
vegetable salads help us to rationalize our indulgences—cabbage
slaw, brussels sprout slaw, broccoli, roasted cauliflower, endive, red
leaf, beet, and string bean adorn the long buffet. As the evening wears
on, the scene begins to resemble a Fellini movie. Loud music necessi-
tates loud voices, and the collage of outfits make for an eye-popping
tableau. Beige floor length *djellabas* (bought home from Morocco of
course), red and gold saris, Palestinian keffiyeh, pink silk harem pants,
black jeans, blue jeans, denim work pants, overalls, black T-shirts,
sweatshirts, newsboy caps, berets, and fedoras festoon the room. I am

the only one wearing a skirt, a red wool short one, with black tights, a snug V-neck sweater, and tall leather boots. Sonya has on flowing blue Thai fisherman pants, a bright orange and red Indian print top and a midnight blue velvet hat that brings out the blue in her eyes and reminds me of my father's velvet tallis bag. Feet are bare or in socks in the "no shoes" house.

The 1920s house is a style with which I will become intimate over the years: a Berkeley Craftsman. The Craftsman style brings nature into the home, following a school of architectural design made popular by the company of Green and Green, which in turn followed in the footsteps of Frank Lloyd Wright and Bernard Maybeck. Rich wood panels run halfway up the walls of Suze's home, exposed beams give height to ceilings, and wood sashed windows don't rattle in the wind. An imposing tiled fireplace topped by a thick wooden mantle graces the living room. Outside, wood shingles are covered with a thin layer of moss. Warm, gold light glowing from glass sconces is a veritable invitation to curl up with a book. *I could live here forever*, I think. These are the houses I passed when I first walked from Regent Street to meet Cloud, the houses that sparked my curiosity about the lives inside. The houses that, in their dignity and self-containment, evoke not a small amount of jealousy. Can you call a house self-satisfied? The whole of it, the cozy golden light, the warmth of the redwood shingles, the gracious rooms, all telegraphed contentment. Could I ever afford, and then create a life, in such a bucolic setting? I may have come to Berkeley to change the world, but the idea of living comfortably in cozy rooms with flower and vegetable gardens is a strong seduction to succeed in the material world. How much money does it take to acquire such a home, to build such a life? My intuition warns me that it is beyond the pay grade of a poet.

The house may not be as large or grand as Derby Street, but it doesn't have a menagerie of characters cycling in and out. This is the home of a couple, of Suze and Nevin, and it is the most "adult" house I've visited since I arrived in Berkeley. Not a whiff of student poverty, or the crumbling mess of our falling-down house on McGee Street. Everything is neat, clean, tidy. Actual curtains on the windows, not sarongs or, as my mother would say, *shmatas*. Fancy carpets cover the hardwood floors, and a clean, tiled kitchen with a dishwasher and two ovens allows space for creating elaborate meals. I'm not sure how the two women pay their bills, but I am pretty sure it isn't on their miniscule salary working the counter at the Buttercup Bakery.

After the blessing (chanted flawlessly by Suze) and lighting of Hanukkiah, someone cranks up the already loud music. Sweatshirts, flannel shirts, fleece vests, and down jackets are tossed haphazardly on the couch, chairs, and floor. It is the season of *Saturday Night Fever* and the Bee Gees and Cris Williamson and Meg Christian. Women dance alone, swaying to an inner music, together, close and not close, and in groups.

Sonya and I, full of latkes, homemade apple sauce, and sour cream, dance fast and then slow, stopping to greet a woman in harem pants. "Brownie?" she asks.

"Have you ever..." I whisper to Sonya.

"Oh yes. Pot is great when you bake it. Just don't eat too much."

"What's the right amount?" We are dancing to "Waterfall" by Cris Williamson, a dreamy love song that is working its magic.

"One small one but no more." Sonya laughs her musical laugh.

"Okay..." I pop a brownie in my mouth, the chocolate the perfect finish to latkes and salads.

Sonya scarfs her small brownie and wanders off to get drinks. I dance alone. for a bit, then head outside to look for Sonya.

On the porch, no Sonya. My thoughts whir like mixed fruit in a blender. And my insides balk at everything I've just thrown at them; greasy latkes, sour cream, broccoli slaw, roasted brussels sprouts, and a chocolate pot brownie. Ouch! My stomach yells at the task of digestion. I should leave, go home. The idea of lying supine on my cozy bed is suddenly palpable. Taking a load off my body, resting, sounds as appealing as jumping into a pond on a hot afternoon. I edge back toward the door to get my coat, but change my mind when two women start building a bonfire.

Thoughts spin, but my body is tired, and I can't quite square the two. Go or stay? The fire takes off, wood crackling, sparks flying. Shivering in the cold night, my thoughts grow dark: Am I happy? Could I ever be happy? Will becoming a writer make me happy? Am I getting too old to be happy? Is happiness reserved for children? Have I seen too much, suffered too much, lost too much? Is this dance between men and women just a way to avoid being accountable, honest? Just a way to keep my life skimming along the surface? If I don't get involved no one will really know me, right? Because who really does know me? Sonya knows me on one level. Or, she knows what I share, the hiking Jewish woman I am with her. Jake knows me as the poet, the playful, band cheerleader, and loyal friend. Cloud knows me, but sometimes I think she sees what she wants to see: a budding poet with an open mind. There's so much she doesn't know! Even my mother, wrapped up in her own grief, never knew me.

Captivated by the fire blazing in a ring in the middle of the yard, I think, really, the only person who ever knew me was my father. He knew all my sides: the side that wanted to be close, to have fun together, but also the side that was studious, and serious. Because wasn't he the same? A man on a mission? Loved his family, but his work was his world. Did he see this in me? Did he recognize the same drive in me? And what if, sometimes, our work was our world, even if it doesn't always make us happy? Is happiness overrated? The blender of thoughts whirrs, when Sonya returns with cold waters, and we dance with each other, we dance with other women. We keep half an eye out for each other, not in a possessive way, but in an "Are you having a good time?" way, until, coming out of the bathroom, a sexy redhead named Claudia, whom I had danced with to "Giant Step" by Taj Mahal, grabs me and plants a fat kiss on my mouth. I wasn't used to being blindsided, but for some reason I'm into it. Is that the brownie?

My heart racing, throat numb, and no Sonya around, I step back outside into the dark backyard for fresh air. The fire is roaring now, and more women are gathered. Did they eat the brownies too? A tiny, waning moon travels over the Berkeley hills to the east. My body pulses from the music, from Claudia's kiss, from the thought blender. The air, piney fresh and salty, wins a spot as the cleanest air I'd ever breathed within city limits. I want to find Sonya, to revel in this moment, but for some reason I am rooted. I am riveted by the contrast of cool air and hot flames. I wonder if I will ever sleep tonight.

Back inside, Suze grabs my hand and leads me onto the dance floor. Her almond skin looks perennially tanned, and her mouth is wide and smiley, boasting a row of perfectly white teeth. Suze is one of the pretty lesbians. There are so many beautiful women that our community gets dubbed the "Berkeley Beauties" by our friends in Seattle. Slightly tanned all year and healthy from our outdoor life-style, we glow with good health.

Suze and I talk and dance. What's going on with my poetry, she asks.

I answer in simple, declaratory sentences, the pot having dropped me into my body and stolen my ability to find words. Suze is generous, welcoming, a light-hearted Gemini. I don't feel a deep connection to her, not like Sonya, or Jake, but I enjoy her attention and her gracious-ness. Where Sonya and Jake have dark inner cores, hanging out with Suze is like being shined on by a warm sun. She's the embodiment of "Don't worry. Be happy," a maxim of Meher Baba, a popular Indian guru who adhered to a life of silence and inner peace. He was "the avatar, born to bring truth." Another truth, another spin.

At the next song, I understand why Sonya has been hard to find—she's now ready to leave, but she'd been cozying up to a tall, very butch lesbian.

CHAPTER 11

The Lower East Side and Yonah Schimmel (1961)

My father's world is mysterious. Up before dawn, away until after bedtime. Weeknights I get barely a glance. Still, I devise ways to catch a few moments with him. Hearing the squeak of the faucet turning on hot water in the bathroom next to our room, I get up to sit sentry outside the bathroom door. Fresh from a shower, smelling of aftershave, I can catch a hug, a moment. With my father away so many hours, my mother is given the unfortunate role of family disciplinarian. Her impatience allows for little wiggle room. Dinner is on the table at five, but only my sister and I are eating. Arrggh! Dinner. Inedible flounder can only be swallowed with spoonfuls of tartar sauce, accompanied by her poor excuse for a pot roast (having been through the de-flavorizing machine); the soggy, tasteless canned vegetables; and the disgusting, shaky Jell-O that, for reasons I have yet to understand, is required to be consumed before leaving the table.

Her presence could not be less maternal as she sits, coffee cup in one hand, cigarette in the other. The combination of smoke and the smell of coffee compounds my revulsion for the trainwreck of a dinner. Someone, somewhere, is enjoying their mealtime. Ours is endured.

"What about your mother?" I ask.

"My mother died when I was two. I was raised by a wicked stepmother."

A life distilled to fourteen bitter words. A bucket of cold water on a five-year-old who dreamed of happiness.

My father's mother, Nana, educates my mother as best she can in the domestic arts, but mom has never cottoned to the joys of raising happy children. Her tastebuds have been murdered from smoking. Her edict: "Do as I say, not as I do."

The occasional expedition to a movie in Times Square or the library breathes relief into the somber home my parents have created. No time or inclination for bedtime stories, no murals on the wall, no stuffed animals. We are doing time in an adult household, underlings to my mother's and father's busy agendas.

Today, I am not sure if her protest against me accompanying my father to the Lower East Side on a Sunday for rent collecting is because she is worried about me being left alone in the car, or because she doesn't want me to enjoy a day alone with my obviously favored parent. She complains about the gritty sidewalks, the potholed roads, the sad buildings pressing in from every side where my father does his business. But the inside of our 1960 Pontiac, radio on, is the only cozy I know. If there's a chance to spend time there, I insist.

Soul music has hit the airwaves; my father and I thrill to the strange and exciting voices, rhythms, and spirited tones. "Hit the Road, Jack" is still my favorite; the rhyming of Jack and back coupled with the conviction of the Black voice rich with depth and resonance works its magic. The repetition of "no more, no more, no more, no more" is my first lesson in poetic elements and the power of music.

"Keep the doors locked. I'll be right back," my father instructs, heading toward one of the large brick buildings.

My mother finally capitulated. Did she give in because she knows how hungry I am for a couple of hours alone with my father? Did she relent because her heart has broken for her kids who are denied the love and attention of a father whose only family time is a few hours on Sunday? Because life carries him off into the jungle of Wall Street, and Saturdays are for errands and duties that have piled up all week? Sunday is a chance for breathing room with my father, a chance for love. Does she feel the same hunger? The hunger she stuffs not with Boston cream pie but with cigarettes and coffee? Is she as starved for his love as I am?

I slink down into the padded seat, hazard lights flashing to alert patrolling cops that this is a brief stop. All around are looming, tall, heartless monstrosities. I can taste the danger, the risk of housing so many people into buildings rising twelve, fifteen stories high. The streets are an unforgiving, relentless shrieking of sirens, honking car horns, bellowing trucks, and traffic streaming nonstop from lower to midtown Manhattan.

When my father returns, a scowl shadows his chubby face. I don't ask what happened. Scowling or not, he lights me up. It's big daddy— in his car coat and chinos, in his loafers and wool jacket. He is handsome in that big-man-on-campus way; a looming six-one, with a wide girth and pale face with dark black hair. Despite the scowling, his blue eyes are kind.

"Everything okay?" he asks.

I turn my attention back to him and away from the street parade. "Fine," I assure him.

At least he can report to my mother that he has kept me safe. He's locked me in, done his business. I am good, very good.

At the end of Houston, my father turns the car onto a small street.

"You see there? That's the old, old *shul,*" he explains.

A car pulls away just around the corner. We wait until he can edge into the small space. A creaky door opens onto the shadowed synagogue. We climb the steps to the Rabbi's office.

"My daughter," he says, slipping the Rabbi a check.

I walk out to the balcony where the sacred and silent feeling is a dark, uncomfortable version of our light-filled sanctuary in Brooklyn. It is the same, and yet different, echoes of prayers distilled in creaky wooden pews. Small stained-glass windows and an ancient, elaborately carved *bema* wait patiently for the clergy. When Daddy comes out of the Rabbi's office, he's changed. No scowl, no furrowed brow. He kisses my head, and leads me back down the creaking stairs, smiling widely.

"Next stop—knishes!"

My nerves ratchet up to high alert as he double-parks in front of Yonah Schimmel, the oldest knish purveyor in the neighborhood. This time I am locked in the car less as his amanuensis and more as his co-conspirator. We may have done business on a Sunday, but this is an errand of joy, not mirth. The passersby have changed on this side of Houston. Here are the Orthodox with their wide fur hats and long coats, the women pushing baby strollers, heads covered. There, a man haggling with the pickle vendor; here, a shop selling bras and girdles. These are our people, and they are not. I watch the parade procure rye breads, corned beef, and the families heading for lunch at Ratner's.

The aroma of warm knishes wafts into the car as my father slides into his spot behind the wheel. There is one each for him and me, one to take home for my mom and sister. Kasha for my mother, spinach for my sister. We are stalwarts, knish traditionalists: potato and onion.

"Here, Janalee," he hands me over the bulky treat wrapped in waxed paper. We eat, right there in the car surrounded by traffic, Orthodox families and motorbikes skirting around us. Bargain hunters from the suburbs push into the bra and girdle shop, the designer outlets, the bakeries.

The first bite is sweet and savory. The buttery, flaky crust melts into earthy potato and onion. Could it be, that in that orb, I tasted every kneading of my grandmother's fingers, her mixing of the flour with the butter, her rolling out the thin dough? That through the kneading of the dough, her love is transmitted through each arthritic finger, thumb, pad of hand that fills me now? Is it the bland comfort of the soft-boiled potato in its perfect marriage with sweet onion?

These foods are in my blood. Is the sweetness sweeter against this cruel backdrop of old brick, filthy gutters, and the gray sky hanging over it all like a dirty sponge? Or is this warmth spreading from my stomach to my heart, from heart to head, the handing over of food from my father who, only on Sundays, brings food to me? Or is it that this delicacy is as far from my mother's lousy flounder, tasteless brisket, awful Jell-O as Mars is from Earth?

Daddy and I savor our knishes in silence. Do we eat these treats to nourish our bodies or our souls? Did we eat to feed a hunger or the ache of being Jewish in the diaspora? Because as much as anything, this is my inheritance: a shared love of food, of knishes cooked with love.

That knish becomes a proxy for a mother who appears to love her cigarettes and coffee, her shopping and her dresses, more than her family; a mother who, knowing no mother of her own, can only look upon her children as objects to be moved about—dressed, bathed, fed. Chess pieces. But here in this Pontiac, with the windows steaming, here is my heart—my father who takes me rent collecting, to a synagogue, who offers me this sweetness.

CHAPTER 12

Costume Party

While the band and I blossom, our task is to balance the joy of our lives with the pain of the world. Berkeley is beautiful, its citizens angry. Anger is channeled in ways that energize the causes. The various choruses shouting from the steps in Sproul Plaza, in front of the Federal Building, from Oakland City Hall, spur each other forward. And then there are the radicals, bombing police stations and taking up arms.

The first link in a long chain, anger effects change and effecting change is our *raison d'être*. But unlike the loud and angry voices around me, I do not yet know how to "name my truth" or call to task those who have hurt me, in the wide world or at home. Can I be angry at my father for dying, for leaving my mother a shell of herself? Can I be angry at my mother for unleashing her rage against my sister who in turn belittled me? In theory, yes, I probably can; in practice, I rationalize that we are victims of unfortunate circumstances. Whether in the guise of sickness or poverty, abuse or death, darkness finds its people. And not all people have the fortitude to fight. My pain is stored in a locked vault where it is kept safe.

For every one of the angry artists and political activists I hear, for all the outside voices I encounter, I consider my mother's private, quiet suffering, her survival plan of self-medicating with television, tranquilizers, and cigarettes. Simply putting one foot in front of the other, she brought home enough of a paycheck to cover rent and food. For the life of me, I can't see how being angry would have helped.

* * *

THE KNOCK ON THE WOODEN FRONT DOOR is all knuckles, executed in a quirky rhythm, like the wooden Han in the *zendo* on Stuart Street where I meditate. The Han, or wooden block, is designed in the Zen tradition to wake us up, to call us to attention.

Knock.

I put down my pen, annoyed because I am just getting into a writing zone. "Come in."

Enter Gary, or Gary Cherry as we have been introduced. Is he surprised to see me at my desk or surprised to find himself in a falling-down house in Berkeley?

"A bus, another bus, and a walk," he complains, his voice a racy cocktail of high and low notes. He throws himself on my bed as if the day, at 11:00 a.m., has already succeeded in exhausting him.

"Well, you're here now! What brings you here?" I throw my feet onto the desktop.

"I'm off today. I came to rally you for lunch." Gary throws down a backpack and a parasol.

"That's a swell idea," I stroke the top of his curly head. "Even if it was a bus, another bus, and a walk. Can I get you some water?"

"Or a beer," he purrs, massaging the top of my hand seductively.

"On it," I head to the kitchen. "No day drinking for me," I say. "I'm writing."

I rustle up water for me and a beer for Gary. I'm working on a new poem and getting used to the idea that while some poems appear fully formed, others require time to cook and much patience. The fully formed, I call "gift" poems. Today's piece is not that. This one is making me sweat. A line or two have been hanging around, haunting me for weeks.

"A marmot's high-pitched song/nature here, or disappearing."

Going to lunch will give it a chance to breathe.

I hand Gary the beer and tell him about the class I'm enthralled with. Inspired by Annice, my portrait painter and occasional lover from Derby Street, I have enrolled in a survey course of women artists. This week we are discussing an Italian Renaissance painter, Artemisia Gentileschi.

"The first woman allowed entrance to the Accademia, Gentileschi painted *Judith Slaying Holofernes*," I tell Gary. To my surprise, he tracks…the artist and the bible story. Her work has captured my heart with its intense chiaroscuro. "I'm writing a paper on her," I continue. (I don't mention that the poem I am working on keeps bugging me like a gopher scurrying from hole to hole while I am researching Gentileschi's work.) "She was motherless," I say. "Trained by her father in his studio. Under his direction, she became as masterful in the art of chiaroscuro as her father and Caravaggio."

Gary arranges the pillows for maximum comfort, sipping his beer and listening intently.

"Artemisia captivated Renaissance elites when she insisted on a trial for a colleague of her father's, a man she claimed had raped her." I stop there thinking about how, seven hundred years apart, Artemisia's trial mirrors the trial of Inez García, the Salinas Valley woman raped.

We had just traveled en masse to the trial. García, a mother and wife of a Salinas Valley farm worker, had become a *cause célèbre* for killing her rapist. We showed up, along with a group of prostitutes who were keen on advancing women's right to self-defense. If a precedent could be set, then prostitutes would be liberated of the crime of defending themselves as well. Charles Garry, the San Francisco attorney famous for taking on politically charged cases like the Black Panthers, had argued García's case brilliantly. Sitting in that courtroom, I knew I was in the presence of an artist. Despite his building a case for the justification of the murder, in the end, the jury agreed that killing is killing, and García's crime was punishable by life in prison.

We think we are in a sea of change, but maybe underneath nothing is changing.

I am fascinated by both women. Despite popular sentiment, they garnered their bravery to call their abusers to task, taking the stand in courts predisposed to the male's favor. And I think I am being brave! Maybe I am, leaving home, fighting for women's rights, writing. However, righteous anger is an emotion as foreign to me as a maple leaf is to a sand dollar; we exist in different ecosystems, as far apart as forest to ocean. I want to always see the bright side, the silver lining. But in cases like Inez and Artemesia's it is just the right thing to do to stand in your rage, to fight.

"Write me a play, Joan Pinecone. A play with me as the star!" Gary Cherry pulls a face, sucking in his cheeks to show off a magnificent bone structure.

"And what role would Mr. Cherry like to play?" I hold out a pencil in mock interview style, grabbing my pad to scribble notes. Why not write this beautiful Angel of Light a play?

"A play about a gay performance artist whose dream is to become a doctor. I'll play Dr. Kildaire, performing sex change operations."

"Do you want to be the doctor who marries the nurse?"

"Of course not! What is this play? *Days of our Lives?*" He stands up to strut across my small room. "No! I'm the doctor who seduces the other docs in the doctor's sleeping room. And when we get caught…."

"Ah, okay."

He frowns. "I need something new. I need a new play, a new place to live, a new life."

"Aw. I'm sorry. Sounds like you need to talk. How about a walk?"

"Sure," Gary glances down at his shredding espadrilles. "Are these okay?"

"Oh, yeah, I'm only taking you to campus, not on a hike!"

We laugh. "Yeah," he says. "You lesbians sure love that hiking thing."

Gary wanders out into the hallway, exploring our funky makeshift living room overflowing with the band's equipment. I grab a backpack, throw in a water bottle, a book, and a blanket to lay out under the trees.

Gary and I have flirted at a couple of parties. I think maybe he is like me. Clearly his friend group is gay, but I get the sense that he is exploring, maybe even bisexual. He is older than me by at least five years, but there is a quiet sympatico, a silent understanding that has grown around us.

Still, showing up in my house in Berkeley? On a Tuesday? But surprises are a way of life here. Unexpected people turn up creating unexpected synchronicities. I would say that life has been one nonstop party if only everyone wasn't so serious. But we all need some down time, and apparently, for a performance artist, noon on Tuesday is Gary's.

A perfumed breeze wafts in—fresh cut grass. I would stay in this house just for that. I never had grass outside our windows in New York. My bedroom view was of another identical brick building.

Outside, the day is glorious. Since the rains stopped last month, the grass has turned the hills a rich, emerald green. Heading out the door, I run a quick calculation. If I spend an hour or so with Gary, I can still write my paper on Artemisia in the afternoon. But spending even an hour with Gary is dangerous. Time slips with Gary; he is one of those people who pulls you into his force field, vaporizing thoughts of work and real life. Not only is he very, very cute, he is smart and funny. And his work life starts at night when the Angels rehearse.

Two months ago, at a party on Oak Street, in the Angels of Light flat on Oak Street (one of those long San Francisco railroad apartments), I met Gary. Michael, Arthur, Jake, Dorothy, Joe, Tzippah, Tam, George, and I went to see the Angels perform at a funky nightclub on Polk Street.

The night was sublime and ridiculous, side-splittingly funny and ironic. We were stoned, and I'm pretty sure they were as stoned as we were.

I noticed Gary right off, his long dark curls, dark eye makeup, cherry red lips, and lithe body. That night we were invited back to the afterparty by Noh Mercy, Gary's pal. I was enchanted by their word play, their outfits, their poetry.

Gary sidled up to me at the crowded party. When he told me he was from New York, I started yammering about my life-changing moments there. The exalted moment when time stopped as Judith Jamison danced at City Center and about Margot Fonteyn dancing with Baryshnikov at Lincoln Center. I don't know why I thought talking about high art and New York culture felt like the right subject, but it did. Gary was right there with me. "Jamison is my hero. I tried out for City Ballet. No go." He waxed rhapsodic about Jamison: "Those six-foot legs and high butt and long waist! Those arms!" With Gary's tribute to Jamison, I could see that there was a true artist underneath the eye makeup, skirt, and glitter.

We talked about movement and the costumes of Dior and Balenciaga and how the metaphor of Fonteyn struggling to release herself from the confines of her costume in the ballet *The Diva* had moved me to tears. Gary knew the work. That shared history became our private glue.

The next time we met was after the Angels opened for the Grateful Dead at Stanford. They camped it up for an hour while the band tuned up. After that, we crossed paths at a Valentine's Day party on Oak Street.

At the end of the party, Gary followed me into the bathroom, closed the door, and kissed me. It sounds weird, but kissing a man with eye makeup and a skirt on turned me on. To our surprise, we were so turned on that we had sex right there, the old porcelain sink banging the wall behind us.

"Get out of there you queers! I have to take a leak!"

"Take it outside," Gary yelled and kissed me again.

That night I learned from Michael that the Angels, who skewed more hippie than serious theater people, had split last year from the Cockettes to create their own theater troupe.

"The Cockettes got overly ambitious," Michael explained. "After an enthusiastic write up in *Rolling Stone*, the Cockettes were invited to New York. They flopped. They had no script, were too wasted, and all the stars that came to see them walked out disgusted." The stars had included Andy Warhol and Truman Capote. "The Angels had the good sense to skip the New York debacle. They stayed in San Francisco dropping acid, sharing their money, and performing. San Francisco loved them. They knew that New York intellectuals wouldn't go for their wacky, unstructured brand of theater."

Since meeting the group, I had read up on them in the library. After splintering off, the Angels became a popular San Francisco theater group. Their performances were free, with no admission charge. The Angels' lifestyle included communal living in the Oak Street apartment, an old three-story Victorian house just west of Divisadero

Street. Within the Angel commune house meetings were held every morning, all personal money was pooled into a communal treasury, meals were bought and eaten communally. A complex marriage where each member was married to every other member evolved. All sexual preferences were included.

As a member of the Angels, Gary was a bit of a star—a renegade star, but a star. I kept our liaison a secret, like one of the quartz rocks I hid in my "magic box" that Michael had painted. I hadn't thought much about that night or how Gary had found me. Life was rolling along, so many things to do, I didn't expect to see Gary again, at least not at my door! But every day in Berkeley is an adventure: going with Jake to the Keystone, listening to blues in underground clubs, poetry readings at Moe's and Cody's, political meetings, protests, group dinners, rooting the band on at their gigs. And now that it is spring, we are hiking almost every day.

I'm out the door, but Gary lollygags, inspecting the band's instruments. And then he is behind me, shuffling me back down the hallway and flinging himself on my bed. He grabs my hand to pull me down next to him.

We make a bizarre pair. He, in a skirt, tights, and a tight T-shirt, his long black curls cascading over his shoulders, ice blue eyes. Me, in my "writing" outfit, jeans and a button-down shirt and sandals with hair that flows to my mid-back. He pulls me close, taking my hand and caressing. It is the sexiest, most sensual hand-holding ever. The problem is that Gary Cherry has "the touch." The touch is unpredictable; it can belong to anyone. It's the touch that sparks desire, that lands your heart in your stomach, that is more irresistible than drugs.

We kiss, his tongue circling into the core of me. As seductive as the idea of having sex at 11:00 a.m. is, I pull back.

"How about some sun?"

"Not my first choice." He points at his erection and winks.

"We'll get there," I say. "Maybe today, maybe tonight, maybe another day...."

And so, we restrain ourselves, straightening pants, tops, and tuck our hearts back into their own respective resting places, retreating into our private worlds, pulling back from the shared one where all lovers meet. And who wouldn't want to swim in that mirrored pond?

"Want to see my secret spot where I write poetry? The last time I was there, the creek was running."

Jumping off the bed, Gary looks mischievous as he fingers my magic box. That box is my private life, a part of my sacred practices. There I store the tiny jade Buddha Lucy gave me, the polished quartz rock Jake found with a Libra glyph, a picture of Green Tara, my Jewish star, and a tiny gold necklace of a Torah from my parents. "That's private," I admonish Gary.

"More private than sex?" he winks.

"Private."

He observes but doesn't touch the other objects on my altar: a short, fat candle wrapped in a prayer, a silver Buddha from Zen center, a photo of my father and me at the park.

* * *

ALL EYES FOLLOW GARY AS WE STROLL down Telegraph Avenue toward campus. His oversized sunglasses (think: Audrey Hepburn) lend him a mysterious, glamorous air—an air, mind you, that is an anomaly in Berkeley, where the uniform is active ready: hiking boots, jeans, flannel shirts, fleece jackets. With his pencil-thin body and glittery rainbow jacket, I am in a movie with someone larger than life.

Julia Vinograd winks at me as we walk by, hand in hand. I wonder if she'll write a poem about the drag queen and the lesbian. At Bongo

Burger, the dive that's become my go-to Middle Eastern grill, I order us an eggplant sandwich. "Roasted eggplant, layered with red peppers and melted cheese," I whisper seductively, attempting to interest Gary in food.

"I don't care about food, really," Gary protests.

"You might not care about food, but this is different." I channel my Jewish grandmother, seducing him to eat. He smiles, as if he doesn't mind a bit of nurturing.

He pulls a beer out of the cooler, and I grab an iced tea.

On the Ave, past Moe's, Cody's, La Fiesta, Levi's, the pretzel shop, we parade, finally reaching the gates of Sproul Plaza.

"This way," I lead him away from the noisy plaza where conga drummers play.

Under a redwood tree on a wide patch of grass, Strawberry Creek runs, its happy music the perfect sedative. I throw the blanket down.

"Ah, so you write in a fairy ring," Gary says, pointing at the circle of towering redwood trees.

"A fairy ring?"

I look, searching for fairies. I set the bag with the sandwich and tea on the blanket.

"The ring of redwoods, right? That's the fairy ring!"

"Yes, dear," he says, waving his hand dramatically around the six redwoods growing in a wide circle.

Gary slithers down to the blanket like a cat. Intended, or not, he strikes a sexy pose. I snap a mental picture, his pale skin and angular features, dark curls and red lips, his face up to the sun like newly blossomed opium poppy.

"Gary Cherry," I say, planting a soft kiss on his lips. He grabs me so that I stumble, toppling on the length of him. We kiss, the warm sun on my back. I can feel him hard against me.

"Two for two," he says teasingly. He leans back, arms under his head for a pillow. I rest my head into the crook of his arm. We warm ourselves in the sun like two lizards curled up on a rock.

I lean back, suddenly very hungry. I reach for the bag, but Gary grabs my hand. "Come back."

We kiss again, and this time, the kiss is richer, more meaningful, as a new level of intimacy unfolds between us.

Over our shared lunch, Gary recounts how he met the Cockettes in a club when he was eighteen. "At first, I was okay singing show tunes, but that got old fast. I'd met Hibiscus and he helped develop my theater persona. He saw my 'inner Gary Cherry' and christened me!

"The Cockettes loved me because of my androgynous look. The first time I put on a skirt I thought it was fun. I was straight but had always been pulled toward gay culture for the outrageousness."

I make a mental note to inquire more about his sexuality. For now, I'm tired of talking. Gary settles back onto the blanket, and I lean into his arm. We spend a quiet hour listening to the creek and sunning when I realize time is wasting. Driving Gary to BART, the campus carillon begins to ring, the magical sounds enveloping everything within a three-mile radius. Waving goodbye, I wonder if home is where your family lives, or if it's where you find your people. I feel more at home in Berkeley than I ever felt in New York. Here, I feel seen, encouraged, a part of something. Is it real? Can it last? Or are we in a collective bubble, nurtured by Berkeley's reputation for accepting the new, embracing the unusual?

CHAPTER 13

You Gotta Serve Somebody

Our revolution, like all successful revolutions, is fostered by bread. A seemingly endless supply of all things yeasty is baking at Your Muslim Bakery, Vital Vitals, and Acme Bakery. There is sourdough from Boudin, baguettes from Parisienne; for the anti-white bread faction, Dr. Bronner's live sprout bread, Staff of Life millet bread, Buttercup Bakery and its wonderland of scones and muffins, and Wildrose on College Avenue. Co-op shelves boast chapatis, lavash, pitas, tortillas, all packaged and ready to be consumed by us hungry artists and activists. Throw in a hunk of California Jack and a local apple and you have a meal.

The breads, crafted with organic flours, are as far from Wonder as you can get. Bleaching flour is passé, as is industrialized food production and growing wheat with DDT. We eat only food made with love. We have come to the realization that what we put into our bodies, though it may have served us before, is not sustainable.

Word has spread around Berkeley that Alice Waters is up to something special in North Berkeley. It is Chez Panisse, where Waters is employing France's farm-to-table practice. Her new restaurant, on the quiet north side of campus, incorporates the simplest of French concepts: the best seasonal produce prepared simply.

Sonya and I, both self-styled foodies, have been brainstorming ideas about starting a lunchroom. We ask Jake and Vogie if they are interested in being our chefs. Debbie and I will serve, sous chef, and wash dishes.

Loaves and Dishes is born at a church board meeting. We kick into gear to create a lunch menu, fashioning ourselves as the "working woman's Chez Panisse," the humble spot with fresh foods and a low price point. With Jake's intuitive touch for soups and salads, we will offer a simple menu. Nothing fancy but a place for students, working people, and women from our community to gather, be nourished, and relax. Vogie's parents' cosmopolitan influence from years in Turkey provides a roster of simple family dishes: hummus, pitas, feta and tomato salads, baba ghanoush, and boureki.

Within a week we whip the cavernous church dining room into presentable shape.

After scrubbing and cleaning, we smudge the room with sage and hold a clearing circle. By the time a new supply of pots and pans is unpacked, the room comes alive, and the high-ceilinged room is infused with the seductive aromas of roasting vegetables, soups simmering, and cookies baking.

The use of the church dining hall is free as long as we commit to leaving the kitchen spotless when we leave. If we ask in advance, we can have a weekend gathering if the space is empty. The church offers us a $1,000 advance for the first procurement of bulk food, produce, and equipment. We are in business.

A bank account with Debbie and Jake as the signatories is opened. All profits after paying for food and salaries go back into the business.

The restaurant is as close to socialism as my kibbutz life: absent are an authoritarian boss, micromanaging, and clock-punching. We work on the honor system and share in any profits. It brings back all the happy memories of Ramat Yohanan, my kibbutz where I worked side by side with other laborers in the orange groves, pear orchards, and avocado fields for a common cause.

And like the kibbutz, the restaurant is great until it isn't.

Socialism isn't anarchy. Structure is critical to success. So a structure is implemented. Weekly menu, budget, and work assignments are completed every Wednesday morning over coffee. For our first meeting, Vogie makes us all aprons, Sonya passes around beaded bracelets to bond us in sisterhood, I have brought flowers at the market, and Jake prepares by cooking up a soup stock on the weekend.

Unpacking the food orders that arrived at 6:00 a.m., Vogie is up to her elbows in eggplants and tomatoes. Debbie, responsible for cookie baking, manages flour, butter, sugar, and chocolate. My job, besides serving and loading the industrial dishwasher, is to make salads. Our organic delivery shows up with boxes of lettuce, carrots, cucumbers, and oranges. Oops! We forgot to order oil! To stay on schedule, Jake filches some of Debbie's butter.

I pedal off for a quick shop. Back with the oil, I hurry upstairs. In the large dining room, sunlight streaming through the stained-glass windows paints the tables in watery waves of red, green, and blue. Rainbows drift across the shiny floors from crystals we've hung in windows. Talavera serving bowls from Vogie's trips to Value Village, where she executed her expert talent for procuring one-dollar gems. The Mexican pottery brightens up the serving tables. We've transformed the room from bland and dusty to bright and cheerful.

Afternoons bring in the sweet church ladies, all polite smiles and low voices in their cardigans and skirts. Juxtaposed with our tribe, it is an unusual tableau—Jake with her boy/girl androgynous body, us hippies, and the occasional professor and UC students. Six months in, with business booming, we invite Hendo to be our bread baker.

"Suze's been fired from the Buttercup," Hendo tells us.

"No!"

Suze has been behind the counter at the Buttercup for more than a year.

"She got canned for kissing the customers!" Hendo informs us.

"Great. She can work here."

Jake has a concern about adding yet another employee to the payroll—Suze will bring us to seven—but we rationalize that if Suze brings in just a few extra customers, we'll be fine.

Monday through Friday, by 11:45 a.m., folks are lined up for our whole wheat, hummus, and sprouts sandwiches; minestrone soup; and Debbie's mouthwatering chocolate chip cookies.

By noon, the room is abuzz with eaters, students, fans of the band, and women we recognize but don't know by name. My poetry friends, Sonya's vendor friends, and Rick and Joe from Regent Street all join in the lunchtime festivities.

"Word is out," I whisper to Hendo, who is delivering her first sandwich.

"It is!" She winks. "And who cares if the crowd shows up just to cruise the band?" she whispers. After a few well-placed ads in the *Berkeley Barb*, flyers tacked up around campus, and word of mouth, we have a regular crowd.

In the mix is Doug, a groupie who's been hanging around with us since the band's first gig. He calls himself a lesbian. We just accept him for what he says he is. He's got a long ponytail and a calm visage; he is always helpful, shlepping instruments, packing, and unpacking. Who cares who he sleeps with? Many hands make light work, teaches Buddha.

Most lunch services find us sweating, running to and from the kitchen for soup bowls, more bread, and replenishments of salads. Even though we said we would stop serving a dish when it ran out, the lettuce salad with beets and oranges sells out so fast that I take a ten-minute break, compose another giant bowl, and congratulate myself for having had the foresight to roast double the amount of beets. I peel oranges, scrupulously removing pith and seeds, dress it, and rush back out to take orders.

When the church ladies walk through the door, they greet us with wide smiles.

"Congratulations," Muriel, one of the church ladies, gushes, handing over a beautiful purple and green coleus to hang in the window.

Jake and I search each other's faces, waiting for the church ladies' reaction to a room full of lesbians. I deliver two plates: a bowl of Jake's kale and mushroom soup, a half sandwich, and a brownie. "Compliments of the chef!"

The ladies nod in gratitude. It's reciprocal; I'm grateful for the warmth of older women, and they are grateful for our initiative and energy. After the terrible conversation telling my mother that I am gay and won't be coming home anytime soon, after she shouted into the phone, "You should have shot me," and hung up, I've been pretty sad in the maternal love department. I have tried my best. I don't know how to explain my life; I barely know what I am doing. I told my mother that I was gay, but really, I identify as bisexual. Too hard to describe, I just skipped that part.

"Enjoy," I bow. I want to sit and chat, but Vogie waves, the signal that dishes are piling up.

After the initial rush slows and our guests relax contentedly, Jake, Vogie, and Debbie get out their guitars and tune up. The assembled diners' conversation hushes. They act nonplussed as Jake slowly begins a Leo Kottke-style jam. The acoustics of the big room are terrible—high ceilings, lots of glass, and annoying echoes, but the notes from the guitars are like a river, a sweet sound flowing in the background, calming.

I exchange my Loaves and Dishes apron for a heavy plastic apron and gloves and load the dirty plates and bowls.

Jake comes over and gives me a tight squeeze. "We did it! We are working, we are creating, we are changing the world!" With a tear in my eye, I slap her a high five and finish loading the dishwasher.

CHAPTER 14

The Berkeley Revolution

In the falling-down house, the Berkeley Women's Music Collective gets serious. The band's popularity is growing. They are being invited to gigs around the country, and I have been asked to recite my poetry to their music.

We are developing strong, outside voices for singing and reciting poetry, using them to speak out against injustice. At Derby Street, our women friends are making films, having art exhibits, and designing feminist theory. We become thinkers, teachers, philosophers, and activists, and we are voluble and everywhere. We *are* the Berkeley Revolution. The moment is about doing whatever it takes to expand women's rights (and all human rights). Chains are broken, conventions tossed. We don't just want changes in a woman's right to choose, the ERA, and an end to discrimination, we want an end to capitalism. We want all the rights to our bodies. We want to make sure every child is fed, whether Black, white, Latino, Native American, Asian. We want to smash the glass ceiling, and we want our voices heard—loud!

We are not the ones with the diatribes; we are the ones with love and passion and art, we are fighting for our souls ignited with sparks that are not about blame but about making things right. We're meditating and marching, cooking and feeding, writing and playing. Every moment feels like a step toward something—a new lyric, a fresh stanza, a manifesto. We are beginning to taste empowerment. It's inching closer, and it is sweet. Sweet in the way of a peach in summer: planted, sown, and nurtured by our own hands.

The political climate informs the songs the band writes and works its way into my poems. There is a hunger for art, music, film, and books that mirror our new experiences. And so, we are inventing our culture, our tunes, our rallying cries.

We are not only hitting the right chords; we hit a nerve. The nerve of pent-up demand for voices that speak the truth of millions of women around the world who have changed their lives, tossed convention, tossed wedding rings, and marched straight into each other's arms. Of the women who stay with men, they add their voices to the demand for autonomy and agency.

I am surviving on a steady diet of music, poetry, and art, crossing boundaries and borders to Berkeley from all over the globe. I am an enthusiastic student in the school of my own design; Berkeley is my school of life. The DNA of the city that is forever innovating, investigating, becomes part of my own DNA.

CHAPTER 15

Los Federales

All fog can be perilous. Shrouding drivers in spectral clouds of smoky tendrils, disorienting time and space: it is a hazard of coastal life. Ground fog is particularly insidious. With a propensity to swirl and shapeshift low to the road, its blanket, tucked in for miles and miles, can cause noon to turn nocturnal. At night, headlights are swallowed in a shadowy swirl of vapor. An epic, twenty-car pileup on Highway Five has already dominated the news this past winter.

Jake, Debbie, and I are driving to the Central California Women's Facility prison in Chowchilla, California. We are packed into Debbie's funky 1940s Ford pickup with a wooden house built onto the truck's bed.

There is only one place to sit and that is in front with the driver. I'm on high alert while Jake and Debbie review the setlist, watching fog drift this way and that, coming in so close at times that it seems we're underwater.

"'The Bloods,'" Debbie starts.

"'Fury,'" Jake adds.

"I've made a few lyric changes to 'Seawoman.' I've been tweaking that middle stanza...."

"I'd like to fit in 'Mercy Me, I'm Lonely Tonight.'"

Jake is driving, and Debbie, crunched next to me, is scratching out the list and taking notes. She recalculates the time—reviewing once more the list the band sent the prison administration.

"We have an hour," Debbie says. "Let's do 'Janet's Song' and 'We're Hip.'"

"That's a long list. Let's see how it goes because we said we would leave some time for discussion," Jake offers. "This is such a special time for the women to be able to come together as a group."

"I'll ask the warden when we get there."

The set list complete, we settle into our private thoughts. I'm looking forward to beach time in Mexico. First, the gig (and getting there alive!). Anxiety rises in the truck cab as the fog waves, a white sheet in the wind. Jake slows to forty miles per hour, a veritable crawl. Any slower and she'll risk a rear-ender.

I've been invited along because A: I go where the band goes, and B: Jake's invited me to sing with her.

When the band first got the invitation, I suggested extending the trip. "A trip to Mexico will recharge our batteries," I tell my house-mates. After the stress of working hard to make the falling-down house livable, make Loaves and Dishes a success, and make our weekend gigs and poetry readings, we are all in need of some rest and relaxation. And I have my own demons I'm battling. How does a poet earn a living in the twentieth century? If teaching is the only option, I am going to come up short. The hierarchy and bureaucracy of academia are not for me. Raised by a hardworking entrepreneur, the idea of creating something out of nothing, of building a business, is in my blood; I don't have the patience for the slow slog of academia. Am I going to make a career out of living with women, or is another fate waiting? And then there is family; eventually my mother will need me. Will she consider a move to California? Nothing has to be resolved just yet, but the questions persist like a low-grade fever.

And so, it is agreed: we will make a road trip to Baja from the prison gig in Southern California.

We never organized an itinerary, but we have the basics: Debbie's truck sleeps three, and we have gas money. According to our map, we can drive from Chowchilla down Highway 5, switch to I-10 at the Mexican border, and south down the Baja peninsula. It is 1,065 miles (or seventeen hours of driving), but we are game for the adventure. We pinpoint Guaymas, a small fishing village and beach town famous for its lively night market, seafood, and great beaches.

As the fog slowly dissipates under a midday sun, we breathe a collective sigh. Ahead road signs are visible again. The dark shroud lifts. Our conversation veers to how Vogie and her lover are getting to the prison.

"Vogie and her girlfriend are driving to LA after the gig," Debbie tells us. "I thought Suzanne was going to catch a ride with them but at last check her plans were up in the air."

In the past month, there has been a halfhearted discussion about whether the whole band would travel in the back of the truck, but the roof is so low that everyone would have had to lie flat on their backs. So it was arranged to go in three cars. "Where's our tour bus? You know, like Tina Turner?" Hendo quipped. But we all know the band, wish as they might, is not well funded.

* * *

AT THE WOMEN'S PRISON WE QUEUE UP at security with a clutch of restless visitors. Crying children crowd in with family and friends. Their eyes plead for a hug. I'm not prepared. The waiting room is so sad. I can feel the press of financial worry, legal fees, rehab centers, and abandonment. I shiver from the damp chill of the valley.

Finally cleared with security, replete with badges announcing our visitor status, and relieved of our backpacks, we are ushered into the community room where we are cheerily greeted by a large group of women of all colors and sizes in street clothes and looking like they are ready for a party—a casual party, but a party.

The band delivers: the set list goes off without a hitch, and the women sing along when Debbie teaches them the chorus to "The Bloods."

"That was like summer camp," I say, loading the truck afterward. "The women were obviously couples, and lovers. They seemed happy."

Jake, climbing into the middle seat so Debbie can drive, doesn't waste time setting me straight:

"A lot of those women are not gay. The affection is their antidote to the misery of prison. Some butch takes a naive mom, guilty of being an accomplice to a crime or shoplifting, and they pair up. You see those children? Those are those women's children." Jake tears up. "It broke my heart."

Debbie takes Jake's hand in her free one. "Often the women are mules or sidekicks of a drug lord, a dealer, a pimp," Debbie adds. "A majority of women are incarcerated for minor infractions or for being in the wrong place at the wrong time. When you don't have the money for lawyers, you are shuffled to the public defenders. Useless." Debbie looks out the windshield as if searching for an answer to the dilemma of women's incarceration. "For a lot of these women who are gay, crime seems like a viable option after they've tried for a job working in the trades, or the unions don't let them in, and they can't figure out where to fit in."

"That 'inside' you saw," Jake draws air quotes around the word "inside," "was public relations. There was no guided tour of the cells, the locks, the institutional, stinking dining room, or the 'yard.'" Her voice drips with disdain.

I get it. Prison is not summer camp, even women's prison. "Well, happy or not, making do with each other or not, we've done a good deed, a mitzvah. We brought good energy, we made their day." I hold firm to my quixotic position.

"It's true." Jake's tone lightens, if only a by a half note. "We sang with them. That's always a good thing," she smiles. "Thanks for singing with me, Joan Pinecone. You were great."

"And don't forget it's a minimum-security prison. These women pose little risk to each other or to themselves," Debbie adds.

"Not to mention, their mood was up at the chance to meet us, other lesbians, lesbians who care about them, who write songs for them, who go to their trials and fight for them on the outside," Jake adds.

I take it in, the circle of support that we, as a community, have tacitly built into our code of living. By actively going to the mat, to the streets, to the courts for women's rights, for victims, for the abused and for people with disabilities, we've bonded our lives to theirs. The fortunate lending a hand to the less fortunate, the strong to the broken.

To be this close to change, to be able to marshal groups for protests, to actually watch change as it is unfolding, is heady. To be honest, this resistance fighting is getting addictive.

* * *

"We'll drive from Visalia to San Diego," I say. "We can cross the border at Tijuana and camp on the way. I know a campground in Rosarito Beach, and another in a small town on the way to Guaymas."

After a night at Rosarito, we head south down the Baja peninsula. I opt for supine time in the back, to rest and read, and to give

Debbie and Jake alone time. Lying on my back, I can see out the side window, falling in love as every mile unrolls with lonely stretches of road and organ pipe cacti dotting the barren desert. Rushing past the truck window are spiky, sculptural cacti, their arms home to bird nests and small rodents. Scattered on the parched land are the grey-green spikes of the agave, beautiful in a subtle way, their soft color contrasted with the hard blue sky.

Stopping for lunch in a dusty town, Debbie takes out her Spanish book. We practice a few phrases:

Llena con gasolina. Fill it with gasoline.
¿Dónde está el baño? Where is the bathroom?
¿Cuantos pesos por favor? How much is it please?

We practice, if haltingly, over lunch of chicken enchilada plates and Cerveza Pacífico.

Pleasantly full, we continue on toward Guaymas, planning our arrival in time for the evening market but not before. We are approached by a fit, suntanned man with a cowboy hat and jeans. "You want to buy marijuana?"

"No, *gracias.*"

"It's good. I have it right here." He pats his pocket.

We brush him off, Jake explaining that she has been warned by her brother about the tourist trap: locals sell pot to tourists and report them to the authorities for a small fee. The tourists are busted. If they don't throw the tourists in prison, they demand a payoff by way of a bribe. We congratulate ourselves for our savvy, leaving a trail of dust in the tiny town.

Outside the truck windows, tumbleweeds blow in slow drifts across the highway and onto the hardpacked earth like sand toys. Tiny animals burrow into the arm of a cactus, black vultures circle overhead.

I'm ready to move on and have a good time, even if a cloud seems to be hovering over Debbie and Jake. Last night, in the tiny unnamed town where we parked the truck near the beach for the night, Jake and Debbie were canoodling, assuming that I was asleep. A more uncomfortable sexual interlude I have never experienced. Unable to shut out their surreptitious whisperings, I was left to curl into a small corner. What were we thinking, sleeping three of us in the truck?

It's been hard for them. Jake has been talking about moving in with Lynn and her two little girls, and Debbie knows that if Jake goes their relationship will be over. Jake can play around while she lives in the falling-down house, but living with Lynn means monogamy.

* * *

THREE NIGHTS ON THE BEACH PASS SLOWLY but contentedly. I am happy on a blanket under a tree, practicing my elementary Spanish with the local fisherman who proffer whole small dorado grilled over a mesquite wood fire, served up with rice and beans for two dollars. Their coolers are filled with icy Modelo, Pacífico, and Carta Blanca. That's all I need for a relaxed afternoon while Debbie and Jake swim and make out in the truck and talk about the band and their relationship.

One afternoon we hire Jesus and his boat for whale watching. A school of dolphins and baleen whales breaching nearby is the thrill of the day. Jesus is a whale tracker par excellence; he could spot a spout in the far distance and direct his little panga (a motorboat with a canopy) toward it, careful to not get too close. To see a multi-ton animal erupt from the calm water is almost as exciting as a Dead show.

After, still vibrating with the whale's energy and power, we indulge in a lunch of cervezas, tostadas, and flan. The day you see two whales is a day for celebration, I explain to Debbie and Jake.

I don't know if it's that I feel a sense of protection from the local fishermen, but I move my sleeping bag and pillow out under the trees on the beach and sleep with the sound of the waves.

I'm reading *Mother Right: A New Feminist Theory* by Jane Alpert and *A Room of One's Own* for when I tire of theory. I also have *HERESIES: A Feminist Publication on Art and Politics* and "Goodbye to All That" by Robin Morgan. Between reading, eating, swimming, and napping, I am enjoying a solid dose of Mexican life: the slower rhythm that allows space for chance meetings, slow meals and day dreaming.

* * *

WE ARE LEAVING GUAYMAS, the taste of cayenne coated pineapple, mango, and bananas still warm in our bellies and the mariachi's guitars and violins ringing in our ears.

I lie on the bed in the truck, the sound of the ocean and the sea birds filling the small cabin as we barrel up the coastal road. Pelicans skim the tips of waves, their ballet a show of grace and wonder as they swoop for a fish many feet below.

Paved highway soon gives way to a rougher, packed-earth road. Bouncing along the two-lane road north, I hear the truck slow and peek through the curtain into the front cab. Ahead, a roadblock:

"ALTO: Federales."

Shit. Do we still have the pot that we brought with us on the trip? I watch Jake shove a small bag into her sock.

"Pull over," an officious, tan-uniformed officer commands in accented English. Thank goodness Debbie is driving since we never had the presence of mind to add me or Jake to the insurance—nor did we remember to get international insurance. In fact, I realize just now, no one even knows where we are!

I sit up, heart racing, waiting.

"Get out," another uniformed official shouts, opening the driver's side door, his colleague opening the passenger door as if in a morbid choreography of the dance called "capture the hippies." I sure hope the pot in Jake's sock doesn't smell. A gold tooth of the second officer catches the sun, glints wildly. Nothing bad could happen on a warm, cloudless, sunny day, could it?

Debbie opens the back door and I clamber out. The official points to a dark, dank room in a concrete structure off the side of the road. "Wait there."

The three of us walk toward the mean-looking structure in silence. Part of me thinks that we should chat more, show less anxiety, the anxiety that was now beginning to steam off our bodies like hillsides after a rainstorm. A row of hard chairs is lined up against one wall. I shiver at the stark contrast in atmosphere; the waiting room, if you could call it that, is chill and damp. Through a small dirty window covered with steel bars, we watch as two policemen comb through the truck's cab and its little wooden house.

I get the strong message that not talking is the right choice, resisting the urge to reassure my friends that nothing could possibly happen. Even if they find anything, they will only slap us with a fine. We have pesos. But deeper inside, I feel a sense of responsibility—I planned this expedition, and I didn't exactly dot my i's and cross my t's about the dangers of traveling in Mexico.

Outside, the sun glares. We hug ourselves in our light sweatshirts and sandals. Jake and Debbie pull books out of their backpacks. I follow suit. Bored, right? Look bothered and bored.

The police tear apart the back of the truck where moments ago I was musing on the waves and the dance of the pelicans. I don't have a watch on, but after a while in the chilly room, I see the sun sinking.

We left Guaymas at eleven and were about a third of the way to the California border when we were stopped.

The three police officers motion for Debbie. I swear I can see her legs shaking under her blue cords. A newly arrived policeman holsters a gun on his right hip. He checks Debbie's driver's license against the registration for the third time. Then, the first official ushers Jake and me out of the small room, lining us up beside Debbie, who is already standing by the side of the truck.

"What's this?" the officer asks. In his hand he cups tiny seeds.

"Maracas," Debbie says. "*Nosotros los musicans*," she attempts in Spanish. "We were performing."

Whew.

They call over a fourth officer. *Are they going to shoot us?* I can feel the last of the day's heat rising up and into my shoes.

The local cops frisk us. Perfunctorily, efficiently, like they've done it a million times to a million hippies. *Pat pat* down the side of my leg. *Pat pat* on the front of my legs, and a bark: "Turn around." *Pat pat* on my shoulders, *pat pat* on my arms, and *pat pat* on the back of my legs.

My heart is threatening to jump out of my mouth; I risk a glance sideways. The third and fourth cop pat down Debbie's and then Jake's legs, their handguns dangerously close. A morbid picture flashes: the three of us thrown into a dank cell.

The officer's gun is so close I can smell it; the handle, the stippled metal that allows the shooter good purchase, and the holster, its leather squeaking like a horse's saddle. I close my eyes, sending up a silent prayer: "Dear God, let us go home and I'll never go off half-cocked again!"

By some miracle or act of God, the cop frisking Jake does not register the bump in her left sock. Willing myself to breathe quietly and calmly, we are shuffled back into the cold room. This time, I realize that it is locked—from outside. Is this the prison?

My body is in paroxysm, the urges to pee or vomit competing: nausea, relief, nausea, relief, my organs fighting a rush of chemicals and violently rebelling. I think we just might be out of the woods but here we are, locked in a small, dank room. Are they plotting? Can they frame us despite the lack of evidence? Can I call my mother?

Through the bars, the sky turns pink with a soft sunset. The minutes tick and time begins to lose meaning. With the chemicals rushing and my mind racing, I don't pretend to read. I lean my head against the back of the chair, close my eyes. In a few moments, I drift into a meditation where I find myself lobbying God: if we get out of here, I'll never smoke pot again. If we get out of here, I'll never drive in Mexico again. If we get out of here, I'll be a better Jew, I'll help the poor, I'll do more.

Finally, without fanfare, the officers pile back into their car and peel off, kicking up a whorl of dust.

The first officer, the one who initially stopped us, opens the door. Without words, he waves us toward the truck, his face set in a disdainful frown.

I climb in the back, head pounding, mouth dry, and my body about to explode with relief.

* * *

"...A LITTLE EXCITEMENT." I'm in the living room at Derby Street a few days later, telling Jane and Karen about the police, the excruciatingly long stop, the pot in Jake's sock.

"You goofball," Jane chastises. "You're lucky you didn't land in a hole of a prison!"

"Nah," I counter, "we would have gotten slapped with some ridiculous fine. Which would have been a challenge, but—"

"Fine? I don't think so," Karen exclaims.

"Oh yeah," Jane adds. "Harassing Americans is their hobby. Throwing hippies in jail and letting them rot is as much fun as a good poker game. Happens all the time. Happened to Roger, that guy who plays bass in Joy of Cooking? Road trip with his pals, stopped. They found a bag of weed in the car. Roger said they didn't take anything with them. It was planted when they stopped in some town for dinner."

A wave of shame sparks, my face hot with my naivete. "Yikes!" I think back to the lunch stop in the dusty town, the guy trying to sell us drugs. "I was scared. I was afraid they might try to frame us…but when they didn't catch the pot in Jake's sock…."

"At some point, you're going to have to lose your white privilege, Joan Pinecone. You may be white in Berkeley, white in California, but when you go South you're in their house. House rules," Jane chastises.

Jane was right—I assumed, *Hey, three white girls. What could happen?*

I leave Derby Street, a full moon calling me to wake the fuck up.

There and then I thank God, the moon, and all the planets for bringing us home safely. Privilege. I'd never considered it before. I drive home to the falling-down house on McGee Street, reflecting on the trip and my near fatal denial.

CHAPTER 16

Spring Picnic

The celebration of spring is an ancient tradition. Warmth returns to the Northern Hemisphere, bulbs pop, hormones rage, and roses bloom. Maypoles, kissing booths, flower wreaths, and garden parties abound. In Japan, a unique festival is devoted to gazing at cherry blossoms. Hanami celebrates the gorgeous, transitory burst, a veritable snowstorm of pale petals. Sappho celebrated spring; Greeks, Celts, and of course the Judeo-Christians have their own traditions. Now, we in Berkeley will reinvent spring, giving it a new twist, a flavor it has never known.

With alacrity, we hatch plans for an outrageous spring afternoon.

Although the Bay Area does not suffer harsh winters, we are just as happy to toss the jackets, sweaters, and scarves into the dark corner of the closet. In T-shirts and shorts, I can't help but stop to admire the showy gardens: purple and white azaleas, hot pink rhododendrons, yellow sour grass, wildflowers, orange poppies, multi-colored tulips, and a wild profusion of roses. On Telegraph Avenue young women walk to school holding a single daffodil, a Berkeley ritual.

Spring around the world often passes too quickly, its beautiful moment a memory before the heat and humidity of summer take charge. But in Berkeley spring is stretched out: a delicious piece of saltwater taffy, all sweetness and joy. Starting gently in late February, cherry trees and freesias bloom, white and pink petals waking up the senses. By March, bright orange poppies are happy, colorful surprises, and by early April the blooming begins in earnest. Yellow and purple wild irises, Chinese houses, yellow and blue lupine, hellebore, and penstemon transport us to a magical world of life in miniature.

Wildflower hikes are organized with religious zeal. By May the early wildflowers are dried up. Summer is on the horizon. By June green hills go brown; six rainless months and the heat of high summer lie ahead.

Since the Berkeley Revolution has reinvented everything (sexual identity, work, music, race relations, theater, art), we bring spring in with our own style. We conspire to invite the Angels of Light up to the Berkeley Hills to act out whatever crazy happening they can imagine. If Isadora Duncan can pass off her nonsensical prancing in long robes in a faux Greek temple in the Berkeley Hills as modern dance, why can't we reinvent spring? It will be a reenactment of all things bacchanalian, hedonistic, with fluid sexuality running through like the spring rush of a creek, a refreshing respite from the hard work of being justice workers, poets, musicians, and bakers.

Tam seizes the fecund moment to film the Angels in a rare appearance in nature. An heir to the San Francisco venerated law firm Pillsbury, Madison & Sutro, Tam has joined us on a few of our antics, filming us in McLaren Park (where Jerry Garcia was raised and played with the Grateful Dead) and on a guided tour of the found sculptures on the Emeryville mudflats where we posed next to goddesses and tipis and angels created from driftwood.

The Angels comply by camping it up royally, showing up in polka dot skirts, garden hats, and more makeup than a full-on drag review. Gary Cherry, Noh Mercy, and the others traipse up the hill, muscled calves shaking in heels while balancing baskets of fruit and sandwiches like some crazed Carmen Mirandas. Tam has constructed a loose structure of a sort, a tent made of silk scarves and fabrics: Indigo from Japan, double weft batik from Bali and Thailand, hand embroidered cottons from the Huichol in Mexico, wood blocked sheets from Nairobi, and exotic wools and cashmeres from India and Morocco. All around we've strewn tarps covered with velvet and silk pillows, blankets, and hassocks; we've hung woven hammocks to swing from the trees. If nothing else happens, just to gaze upon the oaks and redwoods—listening to the blue jays, hummingbirds, and robins—would be celebration enough.

Like a child's painting of a garden, color is splattered everywhere. Yellow wild irises, orange and gold poppies, red hound's tongue, and purple vetch dot the hillside. In the middle are platters of pineapples, strawberries, mangoes, and bananas, covered with domes of screen to keep out bees and flies. I'm not sure if I'm in Fez, Alice in Wonderland, or a garden party of forest fairies.

Ribald frivolity ensues as Debbie, Vogie, and Suzanne lift guitars from cases and rip into an all-women rendition of the Grateful Dead's "Fire on the Mountain," a free-form jam that is a cross between Suzanne's song "Tryin' to Survive" and Brazilian tango.

Missing her piano, Hendo beats out a joyful rhythm on tambourine while Jake gets the beat on loud. Tam circles like a panther, her black camera catching the action. Someone pulls out a thumb piano, another a didgeridoo, Noh Mercy produces a tabla, and yet another Angel a silver flute. The *pièce de résistance* is the crystal bowls that Sonya unpacks and sets upon their pedestals. The musical effect is that of being blown into the whirling of the planets, Rued Langgaard's

Music of the Spheres, John Cage or Terry Riley. While cacophonous in a good way, the unorthodox assembly of musical instruments and cultures is surprisingly harmonious. The flute flows with the notes of the guitar's chords, the tabla and oud engage in a dance of Indian rhythms and Persian cultures. The thumb piano and didgeridoo float in their own bubbles, Africa and Australia braiding together, coming apart, braiding together.

The Angels, never camera shy, work themselves into whirling dervishes, a faux Sufi dance on the precipitous hillside where we had set up camp. The heels kicked off; velvet slippers, espadrilles, and Birkenstocks are in their place. Round and round they spin, their arms worshipping the sun and its light as they spin and revolve in the speckled shade of oak trees and the cool of redwoods. Soon they form a line, grabbing everyone into a snake dance around the circle of musicians. We hoot a loud disharmony of whoops and yahoos. The moment of freedom and abandonment holds me in thrall until I feel Gary Cherry behind me, kissing my neck.

Under a sprawling, sculptural live oak tree, Vogie sets up a small hibachi on cement blocks: she'll be cooking up merguez and tofu sausages.

"Work up an appetite," she shouts from her perch on a large granite rock set back from our blankets, pillows, tent, and umbrellas. "For momentarily, you shall indulge in a feast! Baba ghanoush, lentil salad, and sausages are on their way!" She calls the menu out like a Renaissance poet, a courtly messenger.

Mouths water as we reach our dancing climax, an Angels of Light version of a maypole. Tam cuts the camera and we fall into piles, couples, and alone to slow our hearts, drink wine from bota bags, quaff sparking water, and rejoice.

On the surface, one might be tempted to dismiss our honored angelic guests as attention-hogging drag queens—and partly, they are. But on the whole, the Angels defy categorization. "Anything goes" is the Angels of Light's philosophy; and that means bawdy humor, spiritual jokes, and Three Stooges antics. Angels' philosophy means men with men, women with men, women with women, and every combination imaginable. They may not be for everyone, but it suits my bisexual aesthetic to a tee.

The Angels are about wanton sex and wild dancing, dressing up and makeup, but they are also about genderbending and shocking the theater out of its three-act structure. Who needs a script, a stage director? Beside the fun of hanging around with them, I am studying the artistic effects of shock. While my poetry started out innocent, even demure, I am watching how the big artists play—how shock, not gratuitous but with wit, substance, and gravity, can awaken the senses, light up new neural pathways, and succeed as pastors and poets demanded: Sleepers Awake!

Spent, I recline in the Bedouin tent thinking about art and activists and the realization that art holds the power to change. Take, for example, Judy Grahn's brave poetry collection *Edward the Dyke*, Richard Wright's *Native Son*, Bertolt Brecht's *Mother Courage and Her Children*, and even *Middlemarch* by George Eliot.

But what about artists and writers who pushed the limits to shock? Ginsberg's expletives and brash sexuality, Kerouac's rambling stream-of-consciousness prose, Ferlinghetti's disregard of syntax. Artists broke molds to make political points: Frida Kahlo's brutal imagery of her broken body, the inside of wombs and the pain of barbed wire, Kathe Kollwitz's protest charcoals, Picasso's *Guernica*, Diego Rivera's murals of factories and workers.

We aren't the first revolution, we know that, but we fervently hope we aren't the last. As far as the Angels are concerned, they are doing their part to change the world by shocking us out of our complacency.

After lunch, Gary and I lie out on a blanket under the shade of a redwood, faces turned up to a warm sun. A soft breeze passes. No one knows that we have been intimate, but today is all about spring and sprites, love, and erasing boundaries. So we hold hands, not caring who sees.

CHAPTER **17**

Loaves and Dishes

"Cease and Desist": the notice on the heavy wooden door to Loaves and Dishes on Monday morning. A chain is wound through the door handles, a clear sign that we will not be welcomed back.

The writing was on the wall. Three weeks ago, the Health Department inspection "failed." The inspector noted mouse droppings, grease buildup on the stove, and electrical problems with the fans and dishwasher. But that wasn't the worst of it. Apparently, the church ladies were accidentally served pot brownies. Maxine went home sick and dizzy and, thinking that we poisoned her, called the health department.

We are mortified.

"Onward!" Jake commands as we turn, shamefaced, to leave.

In a way I'm relieved. "Nothing ventured, nothing gained," I say, calling up an old cliche. "I mean it wasn't like we invested our last dime. We'll do something else." What that something is, I haven't a clue, but that's how things are going in Berkeley. There is no reason to believe that our good fortune has run its course.

I hop back on my bike while Jake goes to Derby Street to tell Hendo and Vogie the news. I'll tell Debbie at home. As much as I enjoyed the social parts of the restaurant, the meeting customers and serving the community, cooking and cleaning were cutting into my writing time, depleting my energy on days I could have been engaged with schoolwork. I'm relieved because I knew that Loaves and Dishes was a detour, a side trip on my way forward.

It is over now, and though I am sorry to part ways with the sweet church ladies, I am not keen on us being shut down because of my perfidy or just plain sloppiness. The closing is a wakeup call: time to clean up my act.

CHAPTER 18

Mildred Jackson and the Cosmic Ray

Mildred welcomes me into her compact 1920s stucco bungalow, a white one-story house on Ordway, a quiet street in sleepy Albany. Situated midway between the bay and Grizzly Peak, Albany is a leafy town, organized into a tight grid of streets lined with stucco bungalows. Pragmatically architected, these "MacDougals" served the American dream as new homes in the '20s, '30s, and '40s for families employed by the docks, the refinery, the campus, Richmond shipyards, and the C&H sugar plant, as well as teachers and blue-collar workers.

In the backyards, homeowners grow simple kitchen gardens, harvesting lettuces, tomatoes, and herbs. The houses, much simpler than the grand brown shingles up near campus, are functional, cheap, and built to last. The "flats" (the areas in Berkeley, Albany, El Cerrito, and Richmond) were developed in the 1920s when a new house could be purchased for $8,000—unless you were a woman.

On the surface Albany is benign, quiet, and calm, except if you happened to notice the John Birch offices down on San Pablo Avenue.

The city is a holdover from California's more racist years, and in the 1970s still held out hope for a white-dominated California, populated by an aging population whose mission was to keep immigrants out.

But Mildred (a fit, aging, four-foot-ten women with a shock of white hair, walking softly in orthopedic shoes, support hose, and a simple cotton print dress covered by a navy-blue cardigan) is warm and welcoming.

"Come in, come in."

The front door opens into a small living room with a tiled fireplace and a gumwood mantle displaying a picture of Gurumayi, Jesus, and Meher Baba. The living room leads to a large dining room and a modest kitchen. Off the common rooms are two bedrooms and a simple tiled bathroom. The kitchen is simple, designed for a gas stove, sink, and ice box. No hallways or wasted space. Only 1,200 square feet, but with a yard out back, it works.

I'm shepherded to a faded but clean brown wool couch. Suddenly, I have the urge to lie down and sleep. For the past month, my body has rebelled after every meal. Stomach aches, headaches, and a general malaise had me in its grasp.

I have already cut out hard-to-digest foods: Mexicali Rose, flautas, and French fries, even my beloved croissants, to no avail. After taking a few notes on my medical history, Mildred leads me into her examining room. She leans patiently against the leather table, a table I haven't seen since my pediatrician's office.

"What seems to be the problem?" she asks, smiling beatifically.

"My stomach. Every time I eat, I get a stomachache. This is not like me. I like to eat, and I rarely get sick."

"Up," she points at the white paper covered examining table. She hands me a cotton gown. "I'll be right back."

Coming here was happenstance, a lucky break, word of mouth. I heard about Mildred from Xena, a friend of my new friend Leaf, who I met in Spanish class. Xena grew up in a family that eschewed Western medicine and practiced homeopathy and nontraditional modalities. Mildred is well regarded in naturopathic circles and is the authority on the use of herbs for healing. Her book *The Handbook of Alternatives to Chemical Medicine* has just been published, and Xena reports that most of the remedies are as effective, if not more, than traditional medical interventions. When I told Xena about my stomach problems, she handed me Mildred's number. "Herbs can cure what the doctors can't," she explained. "A doctor will just put you on some kind of acid reducer. It won't heal you. Mildred will fix you."

"Ready?" Mildred knocks.

"Yes," I lie back on the table in the freshly laundered blue gown.

Mildred taps and listens, knocking my abdomen gently in a circular motion.

She reaches for a device that looks very much like a vibrator: "My cosmic ray," she smiles.

Just before I close my eyes, a purple light emanates from a fixture above the table. Slowly, she passes the vibrator over my body, from the soles of my feet up to my shoulders, conducting a silent inquiry.

"What do you do?" Gently she moves the cosmic ray up the outside of my leg.

"I'm a poet. I'm in school."

The purple light is warm and the vibrator soothing. Mildred completes the round of my legs and moves the vibrator across my abdomen.

"Where are your parents?"

As Mildred works on the perimeter of the table, my leg, arms, and stomach relax.

"My mother lives in New York City."

"And your father?" she asks, passing the vibrator across my chest which clenches at the word "father."

I hesitate.

"Are you okay?" She closes my eyelids with her paper-soft fingers.

"My father passed."

Saying the words, I suddenly know why I am here. I know what the stomach aches, the headaches, the pain are about. The fear of dying is lodged in my gut and Mildred knows it.

"How old were you?"

"Eleven." The tightness moves from my chest to my throat. I want to escape, but the purple ray is warm and the vibrator is comforting and Mildred is as light as an angel.

* * *

WHEN I WAKE UP, MILDRED IS PERCHED on the brown couch, scribbling on a medical chart.

"How do you feel now?"

"Better."

"That's what I wanted to hear. Now let's get you a plan."

In a firm hand, Mildred writes:

Two glasses of fresh carrot juice per day
Flax seed tea twice a day
Beets and beet greens steamed, eat with brown rice

"How old are you?" I ask.

"I have no idea when I was born. I just know that I was sent here to heal people." She takes my hand. "I don't sleep. I visit with the Martians at night."

Mildred then lectures me on food combining and how careful I must be. "No mixing fruit and vegetables. And meditate every day for a half an hour. Too much thinking damages the organ's healthy functioning." She gives an elfish guffaw.

I wave goodbye at the door, throw my leg over my bicycle frame. My body feels lighter, and the pain is gone. Pedaling away, I realize that I hadn't paid. I run back up the few steps just as Mildred is closing the front door.

"Wait! What do I pay you?"

"Whatever you like."

I rifle through my wallet pulling out two fives. "Is this okay?"

"Lovely," Mildred assures me. "And if you can't pay, I'll treat you anyway. Come back next week!"

"I'll be here. Same day, same time."

I pedal down Ordway, toward Rose Street where I will bike across flat Sacramento Street to Russell. My limbs are refreshed, invigorated, while my stomach feels the calmest it has in months. Even my fingers are more relaxed on the handlebars. My brain, inside of my helmet, has been transported to a low-alpha state. Between the cosmic ray, the vibrator, and my healing nap, a renewed faith engulfs me. I can do this. I can be a poet. I can do odd jobs. I'll figure it out. Stop worrying.

But what strikes me as I cross Hopkins, turning toward Westbrae health foods, is that I could talk to Mildred. I told her about my father. I found the words.

CHAPTER 19

Ghosts in the House (1971)

*B*AM! An explosion, or a gunshot, wakes Cheryl and me (dancing to the Supremes) out of our pot-induced miasma. We are in my apartment, meant to be studying for the Regents, the statewide mandatory high school exams. But one thing leads to another and after an hour of studying fractions, Civil War dates, and geologic time periods, Lucy pulls out her bag of weed. Lucy, a Colombian immigrant, travels to South America every summer, where she learned to bribe cops and to steal. Lucy, a beauty with a mane of jet-black hair and a mysterious scar down the side of her cheek; Lucy, whose boyfriend is a heroin addict; Lucy, who steals tiny jade buddhas from her mother's jewelry store and gives them to us as gifts, is our drug purveyor.

BAM! The sound of metal and something not right. I lower blinds and close the curtains. Are we at war? Is there a gunfight on the street? Forest Hills isn't known for gun fights, but you never know. The city is rife with muggings, subway stabbings, shootings.

Ghosts in the House (1971)

Simultaneously, Cheryl and I break into tears, the crash or gunshot having pierced a tender spot in both our hearts. Death. That's all we hear.

Cheryl and I have ghosts. For me the shock of my father dying, my mother's depression and withdrawal.

Cheryl is haunted by harrowing stories of her parents' internment in Bergen-Belsen and Treblinka. Tragedies are a noir film etched onto our hearts. We both grieve, but each in our own way.

The loud explosion blows our doors open. Ghosts, wars, deaths. She is in love with Svika, an Israeli soldier. Death. Vietnam. Death is drowning the wars we march against every month. Ghosts and demons. Will this be the month that my mother will die, leaving me orphaned, alone? What if she were shot?

Alarmed, we sob, and the next thing I know I am rummaging the closets for a sheet to cover the mirror. I thumbtack the corners to the frame, vanquishing any chance of reflection. I cover the mirror as we are commanded to do while sitting Shiva. I cover the mirror to do what no teenage girl does, stop examining myself, my every flaw, a pimple here, a cowlick there, an inch too fat.

Have we been catapulted years into the future? Are we living out our own deaths? The deaths of our parents, our friends, our lovers? Or are we sobbing for the universal death, the deaths that happen every minute somewhere in the world, through fire, crash, war, age, sickness?

"Why are you crying?" Lucy asks again.

No words. We can't speak.

Do we not explain because we can't or because we won't? Is it because we have signed an invisible pact? Is it because we haven't yet learned the words to speak about atrocities, about death by ethnic cleansings, about parents leaving?

The fall after my father passed, my schoolfriends pressed me: how did I feel, how was it? (I had no words then either.) Cheryl never asked. But something in her body understands.

Am I crying for her or for myself? Is she crying for herself or for me?

No matter. We sob with no need to join words to feelings. We become sisters in the sobbing, like children who prick their fingers and mix blood with their besties.

We understand something that the others cannot. We have looked death in the face, we have peered into the great darkness of hopelessness and fear. At sixteen, we have both lost so much.

Me and my sister.

Photo shot in Berkeley of BWMC—new band configuration.

BWMC: Debbie Lempke, Jake Lampert, Nancy Henderson, Nancy Vogl, and Suzanne Shanbaum.

Concert poster
for Berkeley
Women's Music
Collective
(BWMC).

Suzanne Shanbaum, Bonnie Lockhart, Nancy Vogl in marching band.

Cha—in rustic cabin on Vashon Island.

Debbie Lempke and Suzanne Shanbaum record first album at blue bear studios.

Nancy Vogl and Nancy Henderson recording first album.

Outdoor performance, Berkeley.

Sister Lode magazine featured BWMC.

POETRY

Sometimes I walk the alleys
beyond the realm of praise or blame
Where no one keeps the tallies
and none can speak my name

But you, you eucalyptus,
    you calypso through my dreams
    so that every nightwalk now it seems
is pleasured by your scent
(such a deafening perfume)
then, sometimes
    when she speaks to me
    in crowded, smoky rooms
she breathes her soft soliloquy
    and I believe
she speaks for you,
        you eucalyptus.

In true, true
        true accordian
the u-u-ukelalian melodies
are drummed into my head
    till I become somewhat more primordian
and it takes pots of strong valerian
to ease me back to bed...
.... most nights
    a mute Calliope.

to be filled with an
        oh!
to behold her and oh,
to be held once again
    in her boughs
transforming jagged thoughts of them
    to one enduring now.

But you,
    you eucalyptus
You Caliban of trees
you bespeak the eulogies
    that time and tide can't
    hope to hide
for it is written on these
        Berkeley Hills
in such a
    stark calligraphy.

JANET
CANNON-UNIONE
LAZARUS

affair

scapegoated in the night   dancing to....
the moon! you fondle the fire with....
your delicate touch poking inticacies
and teasing deprivation with your beauty
my love!

At the Farm

It isn't far to country
        side by side with
        cat meowing
bringing us a present
of silent body
        squashed between her teeth
dangling a limpid tail that

I pick up
            Hairy creature now a
child's toy
            I throw its
carcass to the dog
            waiting in silence
while felines prance
            through jungle memories
to pounce at shape and smell
            of mouse
once antelope

        she once queen
of the wilderness

LIVIA STEIN

Crystal clear

Suspended in sunlight
waving rainbow colors
every facet reflecting
i dance
how painful
each cut with the
diamond edged knife
has been
what a price to pay
to become crystal clear
now
i am sole survivor
to myself
i dance
to the mode of enlightenment
to the tune of immortality
emanating
strength
and resistance
from every slash
and deep red
from rainbow wounds

JONE GELFAND

HE AND SHE IN DISTANCE AND TIME
Victoria J. Selmier 1974

I put on my spacesuit and stood at the start
    of the obstacle course that ran straight through the heart
    of all the dimensions of distance and time.

We fought to get first to the horizon's line.
    With their inside position, males thought they were smart
    but the going got tough and soles fell apart.

Oh ignoble man, shy of danger ahead.
    If the woman will dare, you're content to be led.
    In space suits you see, all that sex mystique fled.

So lop off the heads with sharp feminine minds,
    who've caught the dimensions of distance and time.

Place wreaths of bull shit on the brow of the be.
    A space suit can't hide him and neither will she.

VICTORIA SELMIER

*My "Poetry Page"
as Poetry Editor
for Plexus.*

Photo of girl on steps at UC Berkeley at protest for Inez Garcia.

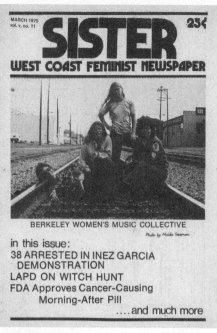

A popular newspaper.

WomenSpirit *magazine,
founded in Oregon, featured
two poems of mine.*

CHAPTER 20

The Beat Goes On

Ajida isn't keen on leaving the Bay. "Black folks don't do nature," she whispers in bed. "Too many bugs, men with guns, and thorny plants and shit."

"But the gig is a great opportunity. And from it you'll get new gigs—in LA!" I yap away in my Susie Sunshine, overly optimistic, business manager voice. The gig is with Toni Toni Toni, a women's band from the LA area that Ajida gigged with while she was living in West Hollywood working as a studio musician.

"I know about LA." Ajida turns pensive. "I worked in LA. Drummed for Sly, Stevie. Been there, done that. Too many white folks."

"The clubs aren't all white."

"Yeah, but management is. Besides, I have no people there. My people are in Oakland."

I'll be your people, I think, but restrain myself. Planning our future would be a line that Ajida isn't interested in crossing.

I brush her anxiety aside. "White bread? White folks? Who gives a shit? You're a musician and it's a free country, right?"

151

Ajida is quiet. "For some folks, yeah, it's free." Ajida pours another a long swig out of a bottle of Jack Daniels.

Our affair has settled into an odd, dysfunctional, enticing pattern. Ajida shows up, unannounced, at my apartment in the thick of the evening. I am in pajamas, writing poetry, poring over homework. We get into bed, talk, and make love. The next morning, after coffee, "just coffee" (she declines any offer of food, always), she disappears for a few days. We never get together during the day, never make plans. The music festival is the first time we will spend more than a few hours together.

For now, the trip is settled. I will drive, she will play. I turn to look out the window at the trees turning gold. It's fall again. The ideas of white privilege, of Black oppression, of racism, and of sexism hover around my consciousness, always but even more so since Jane and Karen accused me of denying my "white privilege." My father lectured us about the Civil Rights movement while we were growing up. "Blacks and Jews stick together," my father asserted, one Sunday afternoon driving from white Forest Hills to the lower east side. "Minyan at Eldridge Street," he told me. "Joanie, it's so beautiful. We pray with Jews from Ethiopia."

"You do?" Even at eight years old, I was astonished. Did my father have a secret life? What else did he do when he left home? On weekends, during extended car rides to Brooklyn to his mother's, to Long Island to visit his boss, to antique shops to entertain my mother, he tutored me in Black music, especially Chess records.

"The Chess brothers were Jewish guys. Leonard and Phil Chess started their record company that gave so many Black musicians their starts. Muddy Waters. John Lee Hooker. All the electric blues musicians who inspired rock and roll. He financed their careers, made them stars." I loved that story of Jews and Blacks collaborating. Wasn't that what I was doing with Ajida? Then why was she so resistant? So remote? So non-committal?

"Make you a deal," Ajida offers, bringing me back. "I'll tell the band we're adding a five-minute poetry interlude." She winks. "Get these white girls some culture! We'll blow them away. And that will be good for *your* career." We laugh for a minute.

"Will they agree?"

I am still struck by how things have evolved during my time in Berkeley; with a simple verbal recommendation, I have readings, publications, gigs. I am in.

"That's the advantage of being the only Black person in the band. I got me some clout," Ajida kisses the crown of my head and slips out of bed.

And then it is my turn to be anxious—performing at a café with an audience of twenty-five is one thing, standing on a real stage with a real sound system with three hundred people's attention focused on me is the difference between swimming in a pool and deep-sea diving.

Here I am pushing Ajida to get out of her comfort zone, but I haven't thought much about my own. Now we have a deal: Ajida will leave the Bay for white bread southern California and I will leave the Bay for a larger stage. And a larger stage this will be. The San Diego Women's Music Festival, according to advance PR, is going to bring together bands from both southern and northern California. It has been planned to be twice as large as Santa Cruz. Ajida will be getting paid $200. I will put on my big girl pants. "I'll do it. We'll work up 'Patty Hearst.'"

"Cameras rolled, heads rolled...." I recite the poem to Ajida by heart.

"And 'Moon Child/Water Woman,'" Ajida says.

* * *

Driving to the San Diego Women's Music Festival is a daunting trip. I know that the almost five hundred miles to San Diego could easily turn out to be misguided; ten hours straight, nothing but a tent for shelter. I don't consider all of what could go wrong. If I do, I will see the obvious pitfalls: driving by myself, half of it in the dark on roads I do not know well; sleeping in the desert; exposing myself to sun, heat, scorpions, snakes. Not to mention the challenge of Ajida's love affair with the bottle.

I fill up the tank, pack, and steel myself. This is good, I say, this is good. Three congas, two in the trunk and one in the back seat, are swaddled babies in yoga blankets. Ajida's small duffel, my duffel, an extra backpack stuffed with books and poems, three bags of groceries, a five-gallon jug of purified water, a backpacking tent, two sleeping bags (one borrowed), four pillows, an electric camp lantern, a foam sleeping pad, and an extra blanket—just in case—fill the hatchback.

Snakes, sun, and scorpions be damned! At the last minute I remember my camping stove and a pot to make coffee. I've never slept in the desert, but I know enough to know the temperature can drop suddenly, turning the desert cold quickly, so I also pack a down jacket and remind Ajida to bring warmer clothes than shorts, T-shirts, and sandals.

Organizing our provisions, I remember my first meeting with Ajida. I went for breakfast at the Buttercup with Cloud to talk about poetry. Wednesdays were our writing check-in: which publications are looking for poems? What new gigs could we get ourselves invited to? After kissing Suze over the display case of scones, croissants, and morning buns, and a breakfast of French toast and fruit, we lingered outside, talking to other women we knew who were heading to work. Ajida was standing with Pam, the lead guitarist of the new band Be Be K'Roche.

"Hey," Ajida pulled me in for a bear hug.

I recognized her from hanging around with the Berkeley Women's Music Collective. I didn't realize that she'd ever noticed me. Her hug was warm, familiar, welcoming. Her size was an added bonus—she was large, solid, built like a Mack truck, strong.

"Meet me at the White Horse tomorrow," she whispered.

On the walk home, I thought, *Why not?* I was open.

That Tuesday night, I met Ajida at the bar. She had a double Jack Daniel's; I had a Long Island iced tea. We danced to Aretha and Sly, to the silly Bee Gees, and Kool & the Gang. We ended up at my apartment, where—immediately after making love—she let me know that she was not relationship material.

"I'm not looking to get married," I told her, even if I did like the idea of playing this out, getting to know her, her world.

"Well, that's a first. You know that old joke? What's a lesbian's first date? Sex. What's the second date? A U-Haul."

I hit her playfully, turned over for a night of spooning. On the surface, Ajida looked unreliable: her inconsistent income stream from performing, her apparent love affair with Jack Daniel's, and living in a room in a house at thirty-three. But in bed, there was something so reliable, so solid, so steady about her. I couldn't quite square the mystery of her.

Now, I worry if I am being insensitive about the trip, about her anxiety about racism and Southern California. Hasn't Jake been punched out in Oakland for being a "dyke"? And that was in Oakland at the food giveaway that the SLA demanded for the release of Patty Hearst.

"We may be moving our cause of feminism and lesbianism forward, but butch women are still targets and hate crimes against gays and lesbians are on the rise," Ajida chastised over coffee. "We can't get too comfortable!"

The trip south begins with a tour of Oakland, then East Oakland and San Leandro, and continues east into the Livermore Valley. The sun sets slowly behind us, in the west. As we round the corner of 580, heading east to catch up with Highway Five south, undulating hills glow in that last day's light, California's golden hour. Painters and photographers immortalize it; Maxfield Parrish, Maynard Dixon, Edward Weston, Imogen Cunningham, Dorothea Lange, Brett Weston, Ansel Adams.

California sunsets—awe inspiring for the view of the sun dipping below the horizon and endless ocean—are the main event, but the side show is just as beautiful: yellow gold light thrown onto trees, rocks, hills, and landscapes to the east, the sun an invisible stage director lighting the landscape on fire.

I want to hold Ajida's hand, but she is distant, off somewhere in her head. No drinking tonight. I don't think much of it except that I like it better when she's sober. Ajida is quiet as we glide down from the Livermore hills. Dusk settles, the road now demanding my full attention.

Highway Five, past the infamous Altamont Pass (noted for all time when a Hell's Angel stabbed concertgoers listening to the Rolling Stones) is as straight of a straightaway as there is in California. In fact, it is the spine, slicing the middle of the 1,040-mile-long state through the San Joaquin valley. The verdant coast range dominates the right side of the road and the Sierras rise on the left. I sold the Cherry Bomb after losing my brakes driving down the hill from Tilden Park one Sunday afternoon and splurged on a used Toyota. In the good luck department, the seller had purchased the car with the hope that his wife would learn to drive a stick shift but, in the end, she never could master it. My luck: Jeff had taken it upon himself while I was still living with the gang at Regent Street to take me out in his small Datsun pickup and teach me how to drive a manual. A natural teacher, Jeff had already taught me how to backpack, how to ski, and how to read maps. He didn't lose his patience when I stalled the car or ground the gears. It was harder than learning to drive an automatic in a deserted parking lot, but driving a stick gave me cred in the dyke world and sealed my reputation among our crew as an exceptional and reliable driver.

I tune in to KJAZ. While Ajida rests I unwind with Bill Evans, Chick Corea, and Charlie Parker until we lose the station somewhere around Los Banos. I am left to the quiet, the tires scraping and spinning, and the monotonous scenery of cattle land invisible now in the dark.

My father's escape was his car. He loved to drive, he loved movement, and he loved going somewhere. Outside was always more fun, going somewhere always better than staying home. Our adventures— Sunday afternoon drives—were his way of relaxing after a week fighting his fights with the Rockefeller Foundation, with contractors who lived for *mañana* and with thieves who stole the copper plumbing out of his construction projects. A worthy excuse for a long drive might be my mother's search for an antique lamp or a new restaurant on Long Island that my father had read about. Our car was for singing. First, Johnny Cash and "Hit the Road Jack," later the Beatles, and finally Motown. Sundays were for discovering just-built housing developments on newly developing Long Island. We would stop to inspect the model homes that the three of us—my mom, my sister, and me—wanted desperately to move to but never would because my father wouldn't be farther from his mother in Brooklyn or face the dense drive on the Long Island Expressway into Manhattan. It was the one thing we begged for that he couldn't give to us: a house with space, a yard, a roomy kitchen with all the modern conveniences.

Highway Five unfolds like a grey scarf. With my father gone these eight years, and my sex life a mélange of flirtations, I wonder if the maleness I am drawn to in women is a pull toward my father; I need a feeling of safety and protection that strong women proffer, but I also crave a guarantee to stick around, a guarantee that my father failed. In the world I am creating, I have decided that women are safer than men. Not only will they give me space to create, encourage, and extol my talents, they won't abandon me or break my heart—will they?

But yes, they can and they will. Still, in my mind, men are unreliable.

When we pass Coalinga, the cutoff for Paso Robles and Avenal, small farm towns south of central California, Ajida stirs. I take her hand now, hoping the rest has increased her sociability. She curls her fingers around mine, and with that simple gesture, my hormones pump high. I slide my hand down her leg. She smiles a half smile.

I unzip her pants. I dig my free hand to meet her warm soft flesh.

"Hey, girl! You're driving!"

"And?"

"On the road?" she says, frightened.

"On the road. What do you think everyone does driving this lonely stretch?"

"What do they do?"

"They have sex. It's a thing. Sex on Five. Don't you know?"

It is true. It is a thing.

"What if someone sees?"

"They better," I wink.

"Nah," Ajida pulls my hands out of her pants.

"Okay," I say, "your loss." turning my attention back to the long road. No lights glow. The road is even light on the trucks that ply this highway with goods from the shipyards and farms of northern California to southern.

Passing placards for almonds, walnuts, cotton, and apricots, Ajida lays back, seeming to warm up to the idea of a little fun.

"Okay, if you stay in the right so no trucker be looking at my pussy."

"Okay," I say. "I'll go slow."

In range of Bakersfield I try the radio again, tuning in to the one soul station within range of Bakersfield. A staticky hit of Marvin Gaye relaxes my co-pilot.

* * *

"You rock my world, little miss poet," Ajida says, looking at me with damp eyes. "Where the hell did you *come* from?"

Come from. Nothing makes sense. I feel like I was born in Berkeley and also like I've dropped out of the sky and because God loved me, I landed in California. A part of me feels like since my father died, I have been living an adult life in a child's body: untethered, unfamilied, uncommitted. An urchin with a sufficient bank account and pads of paper to write poems.

Ajida dozes. I merge left, picking up speed to make up for the lost time in the right lane.

Lighting up the dark night is a tsunami of neon: GAS! FOOD! LAST STOP BEFORE THE GRAPEVINE! Motel 6! McDonald's, Little Sambo's, International House of Pancakes, Bob's Big Boy, Sizzler. This is clearly not Berkeley with its Good Earth, gourmet coffee and smoothies.

Ajida stirs. "Where are we?"

"Closer."

"I'm hungry!"

"I've got food in the back. I have to stop for gas. If you don't like what I brought you, you can grab something there…."

"You got fries? Hot dogs back there?"

"We don't eat where we get gas."

"The hell we don't!"

I pull into a brightly lit Chevron station. Ajida puts on her sunglasses, straightens herself out, and heads straight for the mini mart.

I gas the car up with forty-six cents a gallon.

As I'm pulling out bread, avocado, tomato, and sprouts, Ajida comes out with a frank wrapped in foil.

"Mmm." She extends the frank my way.

"Nah, I'm good."

"No judging, little miss poet! You're taking me on a road trip, I'm eating road trip grub."

I can smell the greasy meat and the vinegar sting of sauerkraut.

"It's cool." To each their own. I head into the mini mart for coffee and M&Ms.

Caffeinated and fed, I head up the Grapevine, relieved to see more cars on the road and illuminated roadway.

11:00 p.m. The twists and turns of the Grapevine challenge my skill as an urban driver, but I focus, winding through the San Jacinto mountains, curving up, pushing the little four-cylinder Toyota to its limit before a long coast down, the road ever winding. Trucks hauling on the right and speed demons on my left, I finally see the outskirts of LA laid out before me like a glittering ball gown.

"Impressive," Ajida says, letting out a deep breath as we are dumped into the glare of suburban LA. Two more hours to San Diego. I'm bone tired but thankfully Ajida is awake and is now playing DJ with the hip LA radio stations. My eyes burn, but I push on.

Finally, we are in the home of Ajida's friends. After a hot shower and a dead sleep, we wake up in a sun-soaked house of three very blonde, very fit lesbians who—at the behest of Virginia, Toni Toni Toni's lead guitarist—have invited us for the night. Tempting as it is to hang out by the swimming pool and get to know these women, it's time to haul ourselves to the festival.

* * *

CADRES OF WOMEN ARE CARRYING TWO-BY-FOURS, electrical cable, and speakers, hard at work as we pull in late on Friday morning. The camp, as we enter and check in, is a hive of industry: hammers banging on the sound stage, wood being chopped, and stirring at the outdoor kitchen, tents and lean-tos being strung up, ladders carried, the whirr of drills counterpointed by loud music amplified from tall speakers. Ajida, quiet since we left San Diego, perks up. She is safe, with her people.

Enticing smells of the open-air kitchen draw her attention. Onions, soups, and black beans simmer, the spicy aromas of cinnamon, gumbo, and curry filling the air. I don't ask, but I suppose that the huge open space, barren hills, and dusty road are jolting her way out of her comfort zone. Guilt starts to creep in (*I shouldn't have dragged her here*), but now, maybe, once we are settled, she can relax. And have fun!

For me, the landscape is a happy reminder of our drive down the Baja Peninsula in Debbie's squeaky old truck; the low sandy hills and distant San Jacinto mountains are a wash of grey-white earth and sharp, rocky edges, punctuated by date palms, mesquite trees, and tall spiky flora covered by an endless blue sky.

"Hey!" Pam, seeing Ajida, yells out. Pam, her pal from her LA gigging days, is the one who arranged for Ajida to play and is also the one who got the green light for our short poetry interlude. Pam is a wiry, curly-haired lead guitarist who has stayed as a studio musician and made a good life in LA.

"Pom-el-O!" Ajida howls, her former self returned. "I'm gonna stop off here," she announces, opening the car door.

"Catch you on the rebound!" I chirp, ready for some quiet. I'm energized to set up our tent and find my way around.

I leave the outdoor kitchen, driving my low-to-the-ground Toyota cautiously down the bumpy road toward the campground. A few brightly colored tents and flags are already flying. According to the woman who checked us in, a crew of workers has been on site since Wednesday getting the space ready for the festival this weekend. Turning off the main road to the camp road, Flash's left rear tire hits a rock, a pebble ricocheting to the side mirror with such force a hole forms. A short but sharp wind whips across my windshield, covering it in dust. But soon, and without further mishaps, I park the car on the dusty flat.

I park under a low, sprawling oak tree, hoping for a spate of shade over the course of the hot days. With a jerry-rigged rope tied to a stick to hold the last corner of the tent in place, I curse myself for not checking that all the stakes were accounted for in the tent bag before leaving Berkeley. I pump the air mattress, lay out the two down sleeping bags and pillows, and bless it as our home for the next two days. I unceremoniously toss in my duffel and briefcase and inch my way in. A warm breeze wafts through the camp, kicking up sand, the sound of desert birds background music. I rest my eyes from the bright sun and long night's drive. Within minutes, sleep hovers and I surrender.

I wake up disoriented. Was it just last night that we left Berkeley?

I open my briefcase, commence to edit the Patty Hearst poem, read it aloud. Poem edited, lines in order and memorized! Tomorrow there will be workshops in political organizing, bee apiaries, herbology, reiki, and palm reading, but today is for recovering.

Above the tent, a hot sun pounds. I consider rigging up the rain fly, if not for a sudden, unexpected desert rain shower then to deflect the sun. I contemplate the digging out, unfolding, and tying up of the fly. Doable, but not without a cup of coffee.

"Dinner in an hour," Ajida says cheerily when I find her and her LA pals under a tree, slurping on cold watermelon. "Slice?"

"Maybe later. I'll meet you back here," I reply, my voice shaky with nerves. I'm way too tense about performing for three hundred women to consider eating now. Instead, I lean on Ajida, watching the influx of women. Since we arrived a few hours earlier, cars arrive by the dozens, kicking up dust as they head to the flat to set up camp. The car parade is followed by cars pulling campers and small vans. Drivers toot their horns and wave. The place is packed. My nerves are jangled in a way that is new and slightly alarming. A tightness in my chest and flight-or-fight, out-of-body wooziness envelope me. I'm breathing, but just.

"Do you want to run through our piece again?" Ajida asks.

"Nah, I'm good," I answer, my voice shaky. "I'll meet you back here."

Caffeinated, I decide to install the fly, munch on some trail mix, and poke around. Clusters of low mesquite trees and tall sculptural date palms indicate water nearby. The map shows a pond and a hot spring in the camp. That's for tomorrow; tonight I'm performing.

The hour ticking closer, I search for Ajida.

"Sound check." Carrie, one of her pals, points in the direction of the stage. Down at the front of the temporary amphitheater, women are setting up with blankets and low chairs, picnic hampers, and beers. I wander backstage, my heart pounding with dread.

"Twenty minutes." Ajida winks, pointing to a row of seats behind the stage.

I settle in, the wait testing my patience. Band members arrive to sound check alongside Ajida. She is the stickler in the group for sound checks—an obsession that, while time consuming, usually pays off with a seamless show.

The MC, a lithe woman with long blonde hair (did the San Diego house contingent come to the festival?) introduces the band, talking up their work with LA celebs and their recent album. The crowd, ready for anything, is already catcalling and heartily enthusiastic. With the discrete exit of the MC, the band launches into a particularly rocking rendition of "Kahlua Mama." Pam's voice is clear and in fine form; Peggy is her quiet self, focused on her bass; and Teresa is both singing backup and playing rhythm. Ajida's conga playing is perfect, on the beat, and riffing off major chords the band throws her way in an impromptu improvisation. She is alive, more energized than I'd ever seen. Her eyes are closed, but the energy shoots out of her hands like sparks on Fourth of July. Raucous applause, hoots of joy, and hollers of delight is the soundtrack every band dreams of! They perform two more numbers. My knees shake as the notes for the penultimate song are played.

"You're up!" Pam shouts as the applause dies down. She moves the mic stand next to Ajida and, with a short, laudatory introduction, I begin.

"This one is for Patty Hearst."

The audience cheers.

"Cameras rolled, heads rolled, I clapped/you were getting back."

My voice is shaky and uncertain, but I quickly realize that the audience is, to my surprise, listening, and following my words.

"Right on sister!"

"You tell it, girlfriend."

I continued,

"The man… has raped our land.

"The man, like a half-smoked butt,

"Is burning out/crushed /

"By the power that is woman…"

My confidence kicks in, and soon I'm shouting, ranting, my words arrows slung into the starry sky.

The blinding stage lights provide umbrage. I know that I am on stage in front of three hundred people, but I can't see them, I can only see Ajida next to me, pounding her congas and nodding her head. I read "Moon Child/Water Woman," my feet heading for stage right as the last word falls from my lips.

"Encore!" the audience is on their feet, clapping for more! Seriously? More poetry? No one ever wants more poetry! Their reaction is beyond my wildest dreams. I expected polite, respectful listening, not rousing approval!

I look at Ajida. We practiced one more poem just in case, and we fire it off like a cannon.

I step aside after the last bow, bowing to the band in appreciation.

Backstage, the band resumes. I am alone and shaking like a leaf. A stagehand offers a cold beer.

"That was pretty cool." She hugs me. "You're a great writer."

I demur, shy at the compliment. I swig the beer, a welcome refresher for my dry mouth and a much-needed sedative. Adrenaline courses through my body, buzzing me like the pot brownies at Suze's party.

By the end of the evening, I have received offers to read in Los Angeles, Chico, San Diego, Milwaukee, and Portland. Bookstore owners, publishers, and café owners have handed me their cards, asking me to call to set up a meeting as soon as possible. At the after-party with the band, there are kudos and high fives all around.

"We'll have to make you a member of the band." Pam winks.

I look at Ajida, but she's standing in the back with a circle of her pals, swigging from a fresh bottle of whisky.

"Aww, thanks." I hug Pam. I want to stay and carouse, but I'm craving quiet to process what just happened.

Walking back to the tent, I tuck my head low into my sweatshirt, avoiding recognition and any additional kudos, praises, or high fives.

My body vibrates, my thoughts spin, and that out-of-body wooziness is stronger than before. I have never been so showered with love! It feels like I've just been given a passport to a different country, entry into a new, joyous territory where there is acceptance and love, encouragement, and support.

I slip into the tent, throw myself onto the foam pad, and begin to parse what had just happened.

Ajida's drums added so much to my words; they exalted the poems to another level of meaning and gravity. Her conga beat on the words "fighting" and "resistance" riled up the crowd. And my voice, louder and stronger with each poem, was the voice of conviction and rage. I think back to writing the poems. I had been enthralled by Patty Hearst's transition from coddled suburban rich kid to revolutionary. I had been inspired by the SLA's food giveaway, by the People's Liberation Army and the Black Panthers' righteous inclination to feed their communities. In "Moon Child/Water Woman" I had been moved by my magical friendship with Jake, by the nature surrounding the Bay Area, the oak forests and redwoods, the creeks and streams.

It is easier for me to write about the world than about my personal anguish, ambivalence, and confusion. Who is Gary Cherry to me, and why do we keep gravitating to one another? Why have I drifted from Sonya? Is my mother really abandoning me now that I have told her I am with women? I relied on my mother to be steadfast; she is the only parent I had. But I also am not willing to capitulate just so that she can tell my relatives that I am making a good life in California. What is a good life anyway? A straight path from high school to college and college to marriage? A stultifying job and kids?

My mind is jumping from the stage to the offers of readings and back to my life in Berkeley. I will say that I am on a path, circuitous as it is, to something very different than the linear narrative my mother has tried to sell me on. My life in Berkeley is as messy as messy can get: loose ends with lovers, a restaurant that has been cited by the health department, a falling-down house and my best friends, musicians who live day to day and month to month. It is messy, but I am not about to trade it in.

The messiness is truer to my nature than the home where routine ruled. I am discovering that I thrive on the not knowing—not knowing who will show up at my door, making room for spontaneity, for living in the moment, for going where things are alive, growing, changing. Newness is the inspiration for my work: new faces, new voices, new sounds, new struggles, new ideas. Besides, if I leave loose ends, if I hesitate to resolve friendships and relationships, I don't have to commit, right? That serves me well; more than anything, I crave being unencumbered.

I stare at the stars, the palette of the sky scraped every so often by a meteor, comet, or falling star. I can see the red glow of Saturn, the Milky Way, the Pleiades, and the Big and Little Dippers. Part of me wants to evaporate, right this moment, full of love and kudos, as satiated as after a Thanksgiving meal. I want to take all the good feelings with me, not worrying if it will ever happen again. I slip out of the tent, tearing off the rain fly so that I can see the millions of stars.

I stare at the black desert sky and wish that Cloud was here. I think back to that moment on the Derby Street steps: "Type your poems!" Cloud, so sure, so certain. How could she have known that I had anything at all to say? And that first day after Election Day, after the rainstorm and the protest in Berkeley, that bright sun, and Hendo's smile. How could I have known, in that moment, that my life was about to take a radical turn, that I was in the process of morphing from a quiet, private, let's-not-rock-the-boat rule follower to a poet, artist, bohemian rabble rouser?

I think of Annice and the portrait: "You are mysterious," she said. I breathe deeply, as Mildred taught me to practice meditation. I think of Mildred and her cosmic ray, Mildred and her aliens visiting in the night. I think of the band and how much I love their sweet faces and laughter, the way that we mess around but always keep our eye on the art. I think of my father and how proud he would be.

* * *

Ajida won't sleep in the tent. Despite my protestations, she insists that sleeping on dirt means scorpions and snakes. "I'll be in the car," she tells me. Case closed. I leave Flash open for her. My moment of basking in unadulterated joy passes. I'm angry. Why didn't she leave her friends and hold me after the performance? Why did she have to start drinking? I realize now that in the post-show chaos I have again missed the chance to rustle up dinner, and now it's dark. My body aches from adrenaline letdown.

Resigned to sleeping alone, resigned to no Ajida, resigned to all my friends being far away and not being here with me for my moment, I sink into my cozy nest. My head echoes with shouts and applause and pounds relentlessly from two beers, no dinner. I pop two aspirin and take a long slug of fresh water from my thermos. Is Ajida drinking enough water? We'd talked about the hazards of the desert: snakes, scorpions, cold nights, and sunburn. But we hadn't discussed hydration. I worry. I think of going to the car, but my nest has me in its clutches. Fuck it. I am tired of taking care of her! Staccato, short conversations I've had with women who want me to perform in their towns weave through my nighttime reverie. "We have a place for you to stay. With Ajida!" With Ajida? She would never travel to play congas with me. I shiver to think of how hard it was to get her here! If I had to prepare her for plane travel or a road trip—I can only imagine her protestations.

Is this real? Or is the excitement of three hundred women together, empowered by love for one that opens space to live our best lives? Is this about me or is this just a moment, and I'm in the right place at the right time? No matter! It is a wonderful moment. Even if I'm not the writer I hope to be, I have put words to feelings that ring true. What more could a budding writer hope for?

I rip off my shirt and jeans and fall back onto my comfortable nest in the tent. The hell with Ajida. Let her get drunk with her pals, sleep in the fucking car. For me there's nothing more sensual that sleeping in the open air, nothing between me and nature but a thin layer of nylon. Through the tent's skylight I take a last glimpse a wide plate of the star-studded black sky. The aspirins kick in, my headache relents. With shooting stars above, the sounds drifting from the music stage, and the prospect that my ordeal is behind me, for a moment at least, I am content.

CHAPTER 21

Hate Crime, LA

Sunday morning. I hang my head out of the tent to breathe the dry air. There's a hint of desert sage, dates, and pine. All of the desert is a carpet of soft taupes, dusty yellows, faded greens. It's the opposite of the Sierras, with its verdant meadows and wildflowers dotting every hillside—hound's tongue, foxglove, and wild irises, its scent of mountain misery and its perennial symphony of sounds, but the desert is rich in its own way; birds are quiet this morning and the little ground squirrels don't make a sound on their hunts.

Ajida and I are packing up. Back go the congas in their blankets, the tent, pillows, sleeping bags, and duffel bags. Driving away from the dusty camp, I honk to the women, waving goodbye; Ajida is quiet, hungover from a night of revelry. I'm also in my own world, still buzzed from the reading and kudos.

Bumping back over the long dirt road, Ajida is asleep before we hit the Five. Reliable Flash climbs the 4,000 feet up to Tejon Pass, the summit of the Grapevine.

Seared images from the weekend flash: making love with Ajida in the car in the campground, the easy flow of our sex contrasted with the hard battle of coexisting, the surprise and thrill of the reading, the invitations, eating lunch with a dozen women I have never met under a large blue tarp, slurping watermelon, talking talking talking and picking at tofu burgers. Lying on my back, naked in the natural hot pools, slathering our faces and bodies with mud from the earth. I can't wait to tell Jake about sleeping under the stars, about the reading.

Sailing down the north side of the Grapevine, I remember how tired I was when we pulled into San Diego on Friday night. A wave of dread passes as I hope against hope that I can sustain the energy to make the ten-hour drive home. It's still morning, the day calm and windless.

As exciting as the weekend had been, it wasn't all what I hoped. Even though I told myself it was specious, I thought the trip might bond me and Ajida, bring us closer. Not exactly. It was clear as soon as we arrived that this was Ajida's gig, her friends, her life, and, sadly, her addiction. Her hard drinking was a buzzkill, a turnoff, and it scared me. I don't like seeing people out of control.

Still, the reading and sleeping under the stars, under the black sky, and in the desert was worth the trip. The campground's deep silence was a balm for my soul. I never stopped to realize just how much noise I was accosted by in Berkeley—a small city, but still a city fraught with bus noise, ambulance sirens, police sirens, and ambient buzz of freeway traffic.

Picking up speed I notice a carload of young men to my right. My eyes focus on the curving road ahead; I notice that they are veering out of their lane, dangerously close. I hang back, and they hang back too. I want to wake Ajida, but I don't want to alarm her.

I merge out of the left lane to the middle, wishing Flash invisible. Wishing the small white Datsun over the cliff, but no, instead it drifts right, driving in lock step. Something is not good here, but on this cloudless day, driving down from the summit of the spectacular Grapevine, I can't imagine what could be the problem. I think about my bumper stickers. There is one with the woman symbols entwined, one that asks, "Does Your Mother Know?" Another says, "I'd rather be reading," but somehow I don't think that's what has this driver in a harassing mood. The young white driver with hair as short as a military man lowers his window.

"Dykes—go home!" he taunts menacingly.

I keep my eyes focused straight ahead. I've been harassed before: in Manhattan, in Brooklyn, in Athens. Being catcalled by men is nothing new, but this, driving in a vehicle at seventy miles per hour, is decidedly more dangerous. There's no one around, no one to hail. Cars speed by at what feels like the speed of light as my heart—my body—fills with the same adrenaline that gripped me Saturday night on stage, but this surge is its opposite: instead of a rush of energy, it's a collapse. My stomach clenches, my head goes light.

The sky is cloudless blue, the day perfect. Out of the corner of my eye, I see the driver waving a bottle. I consider the exit, but their white Datsun blocks me from merging right. My little car isn't strong enough to keep up with eight-cylinder trucks, eighteen-wheelers, and sports cars on the left.

"Don't throw that," I pray, catching a view of the valley spread out below. If I can just make it to the gas station where there are people around, I'll lose them. If we could just be invisible. If I could just lose them.

WHAM! The crack of a gun breaks the silence.

The heavy glass bottle hits Ajida's window, then crashes, smashing on the road. In my rearview mirror, I see glittering shards of broken glass littering the freeway. A wisp of a crack and a depression as deep as a bullet hole scar the window.

"What the fuck?" Ajida screams, waking with a start. She sees the car full of white men and ducks. "Fuck me!" She clasps her hands over the back of her skull like someone in mortal combat or an airplane ready to crash. "Where did these jerks come from?"

"About five miles back. I've been trying to lose them," I whisper, thinking in my anxiety that if I whisper, we can be invisible.

Another car comes up close behind the ratty Datsun, and in a flash, they accelerate, speeding off down the hill.

Heart racing, head pounding, and fending off Ajida's glare, I slow down, easing into the right lane. "You can get up," I tell Ajida. "They're gone."

On my left, a California Highway Patrol car whizzes by, its red and blue lights flashing.

I drive, my head an echo chamber of the bottle's shocking crack. *WHAM! CRACK!* Shaky, I drive, the random act of meanness leaving me dizzy and violated. Underneath, my guilt at pushing Ajida for the trip roils. It's a bad stew for driving eight hours more to home. I swallow hard, wishing I had a hit of pot or alcohol to calm my nerves, but that's not going to happen anytime soon.

"Those motherfuckers." Ajida gets up slowly from the passenger side well.

"I know! I was driving along, and noticed that they were driving dangerously close," I explain. I'm trying to explain something for which there is no explanation. Ajida isn't buying.

She wipes a line of sweat from her brow.

"You were crashed, deep asleep, and all of a sudden they pulled up on my side."

Ajida crosses her arms over her ample chest, closes her eyes. "And that was it? They threw the bottle?"

"No. First, the driver opened his window and started yelling, 'Go home, dykes!'"

"Shit. Can we stop soon?"

"Of course."

"What if they're at the rest stop?" Ajida asks, her eyes flashing fear.

"I'll be careful. First, I'll cruise around, make sure it's clear. Then I'll strap on my automatic rifle and head out like Pancho Villa."

"Hey, spare me the jokes. I'm fucking…."

I can see that she is near tears and her legs are shaking. I pull the open sleeping bag from the back seat and hand it over. "Pull this around you."

"You think it's okay if we stop?"

"That's my plan," I tell her, hoping the CHP saw the bottle toss and got the goons.

After an event-free pit stop (black tea for me and a Seven Up for Ajida), we are silent the rest of the way home. Sadly, it is not the beautiful silence of the campground or the sweet, congenial silence of the drive down, but a fuming, worrying, unsettling silence. Guilt has roiled over my anger and fear, wrapping me in its iron grip. I pressed her to come. I was sure it was safe. How could it not be okay to leave the Bay Area?

By the time we reach the Bay, I know there's no next time with Ajida. I know it's over between us, not only because her worst nightmare came to pass, and not because of the drinking. Even if she was interested in a relationship, I know that her world view and mine are too disparate.

I wonder how my father managed himself in Harlem or the lower east side, on any New York street where a big white man stuck out like a sore thumb? Had he ever been harassed? A target? While I might not have had words for it when I was young, I do now: he was compassionate. He was ambitious for himself and his family, but he also was one to always lend a hand, to put himself out. Jews and Blacks stick together.

By the time we reach home, I wonder if the Berkeley Revolution has legs or if it is a failed experiment. White women and Black women, dykes and Black power, not to mention a love affair between the two. A one-night stand is a one-night stand. Not much at risk there. Even Sonya and I have a tacit understanding that we are happy being uncommitted, going with the flow. We've always been better friends than lovers and sensed that the couple part of our friendship didn't have a long life. She is primarily straight, and I am more fluid.

But with Ajida I had made a deeper, more primal connection. As relaxed as I wanted to be, I ended up hoping for accountability, of knowing when I'd see her again. As Harriet says, "Relationships have a half-life. Their end is baked in. The problem is we don't know what it is, and often the two people involved don't agree!" I might not have wanted to get married, but her showing up and disappearing wasn't doing my soul much good.

Now, she had a good reason to ditch, to disappear. I'd put her in harm's way, hadn't I?

"No matter what," Ajida says one night, "no matter how different you feel," (I had told her how being a poet felt weird—except when I was around other poets), "you can pass for anything with that pretty white face. For me, no matter how good I feel, and I do feel good at times, the doors are only half open. I go through life 'guilty until proven innocent,' and you slide by on 'innocent until proven guilty.'"

Her truth was hard to hear, especially when the sun was shining on a new morning and wildflowers bloomed outside her bedroom window.

"When you feel bad, you feel 'under a cloud.' I'm not minimizing your pain, Miss Poet. it's just that when I feel bad, it's more than a cloud following me. It's history. It's the last rape that hit the news, it's the last robbery some white people heard about. They look at me and they're like, 'Was it her?' Plus, hello? I'm a weirdo. I'm not a proper Black woman cleaning people's houses and picking up trash and cleaning airport bathrooms keeping my mouth shut, I'm a Black *woman* musician. There's no model, no role model, nothing people can hang onto with that. And, I'm a large Black woman musician. Harmless to you, but a nail sticking up in a bed of nails. I'm not my mother, a nanny to white kids, I'm not a housekeeper, I'm not even a Black professional—okay, yeah, there are those, lawyers and teachers. But I'm not even a fucking bus driver. I'm a Black dyke!"

I hear her. I just don't like what I hear. I know it's over with Ajida, but I commit: even without her, I am going to work for justice. I've seen enough racism firsthand now to know that things need to get louder. We've conjured up our outside voices, we need to start lying down in the streets, keep gaining speed. I'm pivoting, changing course. Driving to San Diego, getting a bottle thrown at our car and suffering Ajida's pain are worse than the two Moroccan soldiers in Eilat in Israel. I know I have to keep fighting for people who have less. I want justice for her. It is a mitzvah, it is continuing the tradition of my people and my father's legacy, taking up the mantle of his good deeds.

CHAPTER 22

Stoking the Fire(s)

A few months later, Cha's rainforest cabin in Vashon Island, Washington, is a wonder. In the verdant thicket, woodpeckers peck, nuthatches sing high soprano songs, bees buzz in and out of azalea blossoms, owls *hoo-hoo*, harmonizing with the insect-like whirr of hummingbirds. The creak of the iron stove heating and cooling is a clacker's percussive accompaniment to the bellowing fog horn warning ferries arriving at Vashon's tiny port.

At the falling-down house, by necessity, I have learned to tune out street noise and distractions. Band practice, the ubiquitous static of our neighbor's radio, sirens, airplanes, buses rumbling up and down Grove Street, Jake or Debbie picking out a new tune, the band's comings and goings, the threatening thrum of the rickety, rotten front steps.

Quiet is as quiet can be at Cha's cabin, save for the forest's symphony. I am here to find words. Words to push deeper, to break past my narrative poems into the aching heart of my soul. Will the gentle waves lapping at the beach below the cabin deliver the missing words? Will they, as bard Dylan wrote, blow in the wind? Cha promised me that they would! And so I listen. And listen.

"*Hineni*," Moses says to God when he is called. *Here I am*. In the woods, by myself, with Magic the cat, a wood stove, and a spanking clean pile of yellow legal pads. I venture through the dense woods, following Cha's narrow footpath, a visit to the water's edge to reflect before setting up my writing desk. My mind clears with the minty air. In front of me, a tabula rasa, an act of faith and a time-honored tradition: a writer on retreat. I chide myself from judging this time alone as "self-indulgent," rather placing myself in the long line of writers who removed themselves from society to listen for their stories: Thoreau, Emerson, Virginia Woolf, May Sarton, Jack London, Mark Twain, Beatrix Potter.

I've been lucky. Until now, poems flowed, buoyed by the energy of Berkeley. The seed of a poem planted itself, ripe for the picking, a word or a phrase. I'd catch it with a quick scribble, a butterfly catcher with her net, a fly fisherwoman with her lure, a surfer with a board catching a wave. Once I captured the kernel, I could sit with it, play with the lines, the structure. The most wondrous part of the writing process was when the piece surprised me, going in a direction I hadn't expected or delivering a turn of phrase or a word I did not even know that I knew.

Of course, I had no idea if the work was viable. Only when my poetry group gave me the nod did I learn which poems made sense, said what I wanted them to say and could go the distance to publication, and which were better torn up and tossed. I didn't dare discuss my writing process with fellow writers, didn't let on how words were finding me. I was even quiet about it to myself so as not to break the spell. Some poems even came fully formed in the morning after a dream.

Now, I am here to face down a terrain I have been loath to explore. I am stuck. Or is that fear creeping around my edges?

Since that first meeting with Mildred, the message in my meditations has been clear: Daddy.

"The stomach aches?" Mildred posed gently. "That pain lodged in your gut? That's your father," she said, gently, but firmly.

So when Cha offered her cabin, I accepted. I hoped that once alone, I could face down the words that had eluded me.

Sitting at the edge of the beach on a downed Douglas Fir, the Puget Sound as wide as its own state, I stalk answers: Am I being defensive and self-protective when I refuse to answer questions about my family, or am I setting healthy boundaries? Am I paralyzed by fear, thinking that if I speak of my past, my father, a dam will burst and I will be rendered useless, a gelatinous puddle? There is enough drama day to day without opening my vault of feelings. All is reaching a fevered pitch: school, friends, the band's gigs, protests, readings. Not to mention parties, nude beaches, jogging, hiking, cooking. Life in Berkeley has been, if not a barrage, a steady stream of activity, of doing, of experiences that keep me anchored in the moment. But the distractions are keeping me away from the hardest feelings, the fire, the truth.

It is time to dig deeper. I might be writing, as one listener gushed after a reading, like Langston Hughes with his natural rhythm and timing, but, according to Judy Grahn, I have absented myself from the equation.

It was a month ago, in the offices of the Women's Space bookstore, where Judy had advised me to "find the fire."

"You tackle topical subjects with aplomb. Your attention to sound and rhythm coupled with unusual imagery is compelling."

My heart opened a crack at the master's compliment.

"But I don't see you in these poems," Judy challenged. She didn't smile as she delivered her harsh verdict, but her voice was soft.

She quotes one line and then another, my face flushing at hearing the famous poet speak my words:

"I dance to the mode of enlightenment/resisting/

"Every slash/deep red from rainbow wounds/

"Great rivers without bridges/

"Orphaned children/

"Walking alone"

A tape began running, my internal voice: I shouldn't have come. Who do I think I am asking this great poet's advice? I expected her to be in thrall with my work, as the women at the festival had been. I expected kudos and maybe an offer to publish a chapbook, but no. This was not that meeting. I sank into myself, willing myself to sit still and listen.

"What I'm missing here is you. I want to see what is real for you—right now." She pulled out "Gypsy Reading Tea Leaves," a poem I had written about Ajida.

"Wadis of waving water…Alliteration, repetition, is all good, but I feel like I'm in a commercial, not a poem. Give me some depth! What was going on between you? What was changing you?" Her dark, intense poets' eyes bore into me.

As I left that meeting, a part of me collapsed with each step. I was embarrassed, humbled, chastened. Judy's critique was the opposite of my poetry group, the opposite of Cloud's boundless enthusiasm, it was anathema to the feedback I'd received at the San Diego Women's Music Festival.

Down the street—a safe distance away from Judy's office—I holed up at the Hudson Street Café. I didn't want to go home to the falling-down house, I didn't want to talk to anyone, I didn't even want to be with myself! I was crushed. I sat a long time, steam from a hot cappuccino warming my insides, thawing but failing to allay a harsh chill. Judy's words were a needle in my balloon, the air hissing out loudly and with stringent complaint.

I was, despite other's encouragement, apparently not on the right track. Judy was right. Except for the political pieces, my poems were primarily visual, my focus on the way things look, not the way they feel. After all, I rationalized, I had been processing an entirely new vocabulary: California was lush with new flora and fauna, flowers, palm trees, a sun that bore down bright. I was drawn to the simplest of stimuli: bottle brushes in bloom, passionflowers climbing a neighbor's fence, a riot of roses, sour grass and the omnipresent vinca. Towering redwoods had become my north star of comfort and rejuvenation.

Getting at the emotional kernel would be daunting, complicated. "Wadis" described Ajida's lips but neglected her terror at being accosted on the freeway; I also hadn't scratched the surface of the pain of living with my mother, whose dark suffering dominated our house. Judy was right. Like "Edward the Dyke," I needed to write the truth of my life.

I left that meeting as if Judy had turned me upside down and shook me. So here I am, a boxer going in for one more round, retreating to the edge of Vashon Island, searching for the fire. The problem is, my childhood has been packed away so tightly I don't know how to begin to examine the pieces. It looms so dark, so sad, that I don't have the first words to begin. I haven't spoken to anyone about my father's passing, not a teacher, not an adult, not my mother, not my sister, not the guidance counselor who asked me how I was doing. And definitely not to Annice when she innocently inquired. No one.

* * *

Screech. A high-pitched cry pulls my attention skyward, where an eagle soars high above. I wonder: Am I playing truth or dare with myself? Do I think that not talking about my past can erase it? Clearly I don't have the power to make things disappear or I would have erased that white Datsun on Highway Five. Could it really be that if I focus on the here and now, I will simply grow like a transplanted coleus, a small plant in fresh soil?

Screech. The eagle is a paradox: he flies alone, but in fact, he is domesticated, building a nest for his family and remodeling it year after year. In the sky he's fierce, but at home he's a protector. I have to open the vault, I tell myself, to see the two sides of my life: that while, yes, I have escaped a potentially sad fate of catering to a mother with disabilities, of being locked in grief, and yes, I am in the process of creating a new life, I still need to face and embrace the tragedy, the loss, the confusion of being a child losing her favorite parent, and being forced by circumstances into the role of an adult, a caretaker.

In Berkeley, I have left so many romantic ends loose: Sonya, Jake, Annice, Gary. I haven't gone much deeper than the first thrill, past the skin, past the physical with any of them. Was it because they aren't interested or because I am closed? Annice asked about my family. I refused. I rationalize that it was because she isn't "the one" I want to give myself to, to open to, to make myself vulnerable. Even with Louis, my first lover in high school, I never spoke of deep feelings, of my fear of losing my mother and becoming an orphan, of the grief of losing my father. In truth, who knew me? Not even Cheryl, my best friend. On the day of the ghosts in the house while we intuited our shared grief, we didn't know specifics. She didn't know about rent collecting, or how little time I spent with my dad, or my dream of walking, holding hands with him after he passed, and waking up distraught, confused, and aching with missing him.

One way to get closer to what Judy was pushing for is to talk about Ajida, about the sadness of falling for someone who could never be available. Talk about the racial tension, the push-pull of wanting and not wanting. Maybe, if I could learn to trust myself more at the type-writer, veer away from safe topics, I could step a toe in the muddy waters of loss, longing, and grief.

When Cha offered her cabin, it was a surprising, generous gesture that touched me the way that Cloud had with her first command: "Type your poems."

Tripping over giant tree roots in the morning drip of fog, I right myself. My mind spins with first lines, threads, butterflies. To buoy my confidence for Judy's challenge, I take stock of my progress, try to bask, if just for a moment, in my accomplishments: I am giving poetry readings and being published. I sat for my portrait and narrowly escaped a Mexican prison. I sang in a prison, fought for Inez, began a restaurant business, lived collectively, and now, am helping to start a battered women's shelter. I am contributing to the movement of women slowly breaking through. By separating ourselves, our finances, and our creativity, we have shone a bright light on the brokenness in this country. Broken are the rape laws. Broken are the domestic abuse laws. Broken are women's career limitations. Broken are the banking laws that kept women disempowered. Broken are the lives of people with disabilities—with few options. Broken is addiction.

We have taken control of the press by starting our own presses. We have stopped waiting for male approval, stopped knocking on closed doors. We are buying land, starting businesses, and shifting for ourselves.

Poetry has called me, and I am answering. The Bay Area poetry scene is a nexus that holds me, inspires me, and encourages me. Listening to Anne Waldman, Jessica Hagedorn, Ruth Weiss, Diane di Prima, Judy Grahn, and Pat Parker speaking their truths is my classroom.

We are speaking for ourselves and for each other. As Jack Hirschman wrote, we are using poetry as a weapon. I might not have found the seed that Judy Grahn demanded, not yet anyway, but I have pushed my own limits! I am exploring resistance, boycotting, Buddhism, meditation, nutrition, socialism in action, and silence.

* * *

BACK IN THE COZY CABIN, I remember Cha's introduction to Vashon Island, about the Native Americans who lived and worked here only to be booted off by the British. Writing about the violent disruption could be another dip into a deeper well, a path to my injured heart.

"Can you hear it?" Cha asked. "This land breathes sadness."

We sat listening to the waves and the breeze whispering in the tall firs.

"For over a thousand years the S'Homamish lived here peacefully." She breathed out a frustrated sigh. "They fished and paddled canoes around the island. They were very peaceful, content. Until the British banished them."

I tried to imagine the scene: the natives in their clothes of deer skins, roughhewn canoes and huts, the Brits with their ships and weapons.

"It was a travesty," Cha explained. "George Vancouver rounded up and interned the Natives on another island so he could log Vashon." I tried to imagine the native life here just a short time ago! She went on: "After logging ended, the Japanese arrived. They were peaceful. They planted and grew the most incredible strawberries until they too were banished to WWII internment camps," Cha explained wistfully.

"Fear. Domination. Control. White men want what they want," I said, making a mental note: explore the pain of dislocation. If I went back through time, beyond my parents to my grandparents, the pain of my own immigrant family came into focus, the searching for home, and how their pain had informed generations. Pogroms, antisemitism, marginalization were woven through my family history like the blue thread through the tallis. The thought of being displaced, distrusted, and outcast triggered the memory of being stopped by the police on the way to the White Horse, the run in with the police in Mexico, my heart and stomach clutching, the rage of indignation rising, the bile in the back of my throat. I reeled then, nausea brewing at the helplessness of being dominated, violated. And my people had survived worse, were incarcerated and murdered for simply living. Sadly, the atrocities continued every day, in Oakland, Berkeley, and San Francisco.

The personal is political! How critical it is to fight back, to resist. I thought of our protests for Inez Garcia and her life sentence for murdering her rapist. The verdict was a hard loss for our side and the brilliant Charles Gary, who argued Garcia's case of self-defense. But if we keep fighting, eventually our protestations will be heard. Things can change; we have to hold that dear. Practicing patience isn't innate, but we can learn. Didn't India eventually throw off the yoke of Britain? Didn't our country break free from royal rule? Didn't women at least come as far as having the right to vote? All the wins came after long, hard struggles. The road to freedom is long, but it is the only road there is.

Getting my pads in order, I scribble words: "S'Homamish, immigration, dislocation, expatriation." On the beach, Cha and I rest on a giant log, the salty Sound beyond and eagles above. Part of me wishes she will kiss me again while part of me is adamant about a drama-free retreat. Cha arrived in Berkeley with a tribe of women from the Northwest. Xena, Leaf's lover, is the conduit to her Berkeley friends. They met in "Women and Paganism," a conference on archetypes where Starhawk, Vicki Noble, and others spoke of the era in history when women were empowered, when they ruled.

Cha and I like each other a lot, or more to the point, we honor one another's differences. Still, I'm not convinced that she truly gets me, or if she just gets the picture she wants to see. The cool poet who stands up and speaks her piece. Yes, she can see that. But can she see the fragile, small, hurting me? Most people don't. It's not their fault: my pain is in the vault, masterfully hidden. It's time to let it out.

CHAPTER 23

The Accident

It's 1965. Exhausted from fighting traffic from northern Bronx through Queens, my mother turns the Chrysler 88 into the steep driveway of our apartment building. Cracking her door to reach the garage door controls, her foot slips off the brake.

Left arm out the door, my grandmother in the passenger seat, the car begins to slip down the sharp incline. The car picks up speed, my mother panics. The emergency brake is a pedal she can't reach so she hangs on to the steering wheel, trying to gain control of the runaway car.

"Bzzzzzz.... Bzzzzzz...." I wake up to the annoying whine of a buzz saw and a woodpecker knocking its beak against the tall fir just outside the cabin. I shake my head, wishing I could undream the dream and reorient myself to the chilly cabin, to the silence.

Why this dream? Why now, when I've made space to retreat, the word "Daddy" hounding me and Judy Grahn's critique gnawing? My heart wants only to face these demons, face this truth of this dark chapter and get out the other side alive. Now, it seems I'll have to add my mother to the mix.

Day two of my retreat. Cha is in Seattle at Lorene's. The yellow pads taunt me, the words and phrases I scribbled unfinished, fragments. My body is lead, pinning me to Cha's lumpy, cozy bed. Even if I was light as air, I don't want to get up. I don't want to face the yellow legal pads. I don't want to write. Futile, I think. Who wants to hear a sad story? Who wants to hear about a lonely and lost girl, who, by luck or by chance or by the grace of God, escaped to find life? Why go back?

I stare vacantly at the gray woods, at Magic the cat curled in a ball by the now-cold stove, the rustic shelf of canned fruit, oil, oatmeal, rice, dried beans, and kelp. Glassware and canned tomatoes. I shiver. I burrow. I try to shake off the memory of that night.

I was in the kitchen, on the phone with my father, who was laid up in the hospital, again. His recovery was not going well, but no one was telling me how dire things were. My father's gall bladder had burst; he was septic.

The woodpecker pecks, its rat-a-tat tapping a match for the anxiety threatening to consume me. We were alone, my sister and I. That afternoon, for no reason, she had started pounding on me. "I hate you! I hate you!" she barked. I wanted to tell my father, and I didn't. I didn't want to upset him. Things were not good. My mother, on the verge of a nervous breakdown, had no recourse to my sister's rage, for my fragility, for our falling-apart family.

Marshalling my inner fighter—the one that flew seventeen hours to Israel by myself, the one who moved to Berkeley, started a business, the one who went on stage—I creep out of bed. Pulling on furry slippers, I walk across the wood floor, turn on the kettle, and stoke the fire. Lighting the match to dry paper, adding slivers of kindling, calms me. The warmth filling the room brings me back, away from the dream and into this beautiful place. Northwest summers can be cold and gray, foggy, and dreary. At the moment, the outer landscape matches my inner landscape. If I'm going to venture down the road of bumpy, inner terrain, I may as well be dressed in warm sweats accompanied by a leaden landscape. For wasn't that what my life became in the year my mother had her accident and my father died? Ashen. Heavy as lead. Hopeless.

I sit with my coffee, in the big chair near the stove, wrapping a soft afghan over my legs. My mother fell out of the car that night, breaking everything from her hips down. My grandmother, who had never learned how to drive, did all she could to steer the car away from the immobile body of her daughter-in-law. After a harrowing few moments, and my grandmother's otherworldly determination, the car finally smashed into the garage wall. Hearing screams and the crash of metal on wall, neighbors ran down to the garage. My stomach clutches at the memory of that night, of the terror and loneliness I feared I would never recover from.

I throw off the afghan, the yellow pads calling for words. I was moments away from becoming an orphan. "Car crash. Death. Accident. Helpless. Alone. Scared. Terrified."

I scribble, fighting the urge to get back into bed. Is this a good idea? To open this Pandora's box, here, alone, far away from everyone I know, with no telephone, no one to catch me if I fall?

I sip the cooled coffee, willing myself to stay put at the desk, to stay calm. More woodpecker, a peek of sun through a break in the clouds. And Annice wonders why I can't tell her about my family! It was a train wreck, a war zone, followed by years of brokenness. The accident was horrific, but things got worse.

Grandma, disheveled and ashen, rushed into the apartment, imploring my sister and me not to go downstairs.

For the next six months my mother didn't come home. She was in traction, laid up in a body cast with her lower body, her leg, her pelvis broken nearly beyond repair. Finally stable, the doctors agreed to move her to Montefiore to be near my father.

* * *

How do I write this? My big, confident fixer of a father, in a hospital gown, alarmed that something was going on at home. My grandmother banishing us to the bedroom to watch television. She never wanted us to watch television! What are the words to describe the moment the rug is pulled out? All the guard rails vanish and you are catapulted over the side of road, down a steep cliff. How do you talk about missing your father after months in and out of the hospital, and then being forced to face yet another tragedy? How do you talk about the years of nail-biting anxiety when your broken mother would disappear, leaving you orphaned with your angry sister?

The day after the accident, I walked to school, alone, bleary, and wan. I stood off to the side of the kids lining up outside of the red brick schoolhouse. In that one morning, I knew I would never be a part of them again. I had never felt more alone. I was ashamed and scared. Both of my parents in the hospital, my immigrant grandmother marshalling every ounce of energy to care for two traumatized, confused adolescents. How crazy was that? All I wanted was for no one to notice, for our life to return to the way it was before.

More coffee. I can't wake up from the dream, from the words on the page, to the moment. I am exhausted by the memory of this grim chapter of my life. I have erased it, stored it away in the vault along with my father's funeral, the beatings by my sister, the grief of my mother. I leave the desk, burrow back into the bed. I'm not sure that I am cut out for this, I'm not sure I'm brave enough. I'm not sure that I even want to share.... Maybe it's me, but it all feels so terribly tragic. Why not keep it under the rug so I can move on with my life?

* * *

It rained all the way to the hospital. In the silent car, I could sense the weight of the moment on the shoulders of my uncle and grandmother. What could they say to my sister and me in the back seat? *We don't know if either of them will make it. Your father's gall bladder burst and he is going to die. Your mother's lungs were damaged in the accident. We don't know if she'll walk again.*

In the meantime, my grandmother was the boss of us, or she was trying. A Polish immigrant, a seamstress and tough as nails, she was out of her ken with my sister and me, two rock and roll loving kids in middle class Forest Hills.

At Montefiore, the hallway overflowed with my parents' friends. I stood by the window at the end of the hallway, watching rain drip in dirty rivulets down the scratched pane. My throat was tight and getting tighter. In the room with my mother, her cousins from New England fussed over her, bringing chicken soup and pastrami, anything to get her to eat and get her strength back. My grandmother was in my father's room, across the hall, the door closed. Finally, I was allowed to go into the room to see my father. I stood obediently at the bedside, my father supine in the hospital bed. So strange not to see him in his work suit or weekend chinos. There wasn't much to say.

"Are you doing what Grandma tells you?"

"Yes."

"Are you okay?"

"Yes."

It was all a lie. In one glorious, swift moment I learned about the honorable benefits of lying, about hiding feelings, hiding truth. For how could I tell this man, whose life hung in balance, that my sister was beating me, that I was scared?

I couldn't. I would do anything to make it easier for him.

CHAPTER **24**

Jazz and the River of Words

"Go where the fire is!" Judy's imperative echoes.

I keep my game face on. The Queen of the lesbian poetry scene has dissed me.

Or has she? Even though I may want her to offer me a book contract, I request a critique. Critiques are good. Challenging, but good. Perhaps she is helping. Isn't criticism part and parcel of the artist's journey? Writing is not for the faint of heart! I have it easy. My early poems had been lauded. Published.

Down the stairs of the women's bookstore offices, I conjure up memories, anything to comfort the blow from the blunt force of Judy's words. I rifle through them like a sad deck of cards. The fire! It is no secret.

Then, at the Hudson Street Café, I pull out my notebook: my stomach aches, tears threaten. I sip the hot cappuccino, the warm milk soothing, when a picture of me standing next to my father's hospital bed comes into focus.

My father was my best friend, the one who saw me, who understood. In his hospital gown, my big father looked deflated. My father who solved all problems, fixed things. My father, who protected me, was lost in this sterile, ugly hospital room. His fear and loneliness and my fear and loneliness collided. The moment was fraught, tense, as if we were afraid of each other, of how close we were, of speaking. What could we say? He couldn't tell me that he was dying, though he may have wanted to. I didn't know he was and thought he simply wanted a private moment, like when he would peek into my room while I was doing my homework, just to check on me.

In Hebrew school I learned that Chana is Shmuel's mother. My Hebrew name is Chana, my father's Shmuel. In those months of caring for him, for his open wounds, I became his mother. When his gallbladder burst, the doctors created a duct to drain the bile. Awkwardly positioned, he needed help to change the bandages. At eleven, I became caretaker, mother, nurse.

The scent of the fecund forest pulls me out of my memories and back to my desk, to the window looking out toward the Sound. Now, on July 13th on Vashon Island, in a tiny wooden shack, I beg the trees, the woodpecker, the owl, the hummingbirds, the waves, the whales, the dolphins, the clattering rocks on the beach for words.

I know where the kernel is buried. I know where the fire burns.

"You don't have to share this with anyone," Judy advises, throwing down a challenge. "Just write what you feel. If you like it, keep going."

What are the words for losing my protector, the one who nurtured, who cared? What are the words for feeling different from all the kids with two parents, brothers and sisters who didn't beat them, a mother who didn't smoke all day and instead emanated kindness and love?

* * *

I SCRIBBLE DOWN WORDS, free associating images from my life in New York and time with my father. "Coney Island. The arcade. Goldfish. Hot dogs. Knishes. Traffic. Family. Soul music on the radio."

Spinning with the panoply of words, I am back on those bumper cars or spinning cups. How to put it all together? Standing in the portal of the creaky wooden door, the sun peeks out from under thick cloud cover. I grab my jacket, pad, and pen and step onto the soft loam to grab a bit of sun, to change my view, hoping that maybe, just maybe, the early afternoon sun's warmth will illuminate that path, will light up the sentence, will open the door.

Down by the water's edge, someone has left a low canvas beach chair. I wheel around, wondering who might be hoping for a nice sit after their beachcombing. No one. I set myself down, turning my face up to the sun.

In the quiet moment, I decide it is as good a time as any to meditate, if only for a few minutes. This morning's trouble making a fire distracted me from my sitting routine. I fold my hands, beginning the practice of clearing my thoughts. Judy's words echo, the memory of my father's round and cheerful face, his blue eyes drift in and out like a cool spring in a desert: a mirage, I feel the images, the past closing in, my chest heavy, air passageways tightening, I unfold myself from the low chair, determined to chain myself to that desk until I find the words. Back up the hill, in the shade of a tall fir, a dream from long ago spins.

It is the fall after my father passed. I am on a dark street, at night, walking with my father, my hand in his hand.

When I wake up, I am distraught. How did he come to me? What does this mean? I tell no one.

"It was you who led me by my small hand, handing me the midnight-blue tallis bag," I write on the yellow pad.

* * *

Back at the roughhewn desk, a wide plank of wood balanced on two sawhorses, I am agitated; the memory of the dream has sent my blood rushing. With that journey to the other side, to dreams, to the non-physical, I am caught between this world of beaches and ferries, of sky and sun, and the world of memory, dreams, and spirit.

I brew a strong cup of tea, abandoning the idea of a meditation for today. I copy the dream, wondering about the next line. But why wait? I'm thinking about singing in the car, about pop tunes, about how much I loved the repetition, rhyme, and rhythm of songs. Why not use music to help?

I am caught on the word, loving it, the best of the list of words. Muse-ic. Music had always had the medicine to open my heart. In the car, singing "Hit the Road, Jack," there was joy I could never express at home; with rock and roll and the Grateful Dead there was dancing and a sense of being open to the world in all of its complexity. Music led to dancing. Music was my happy place. Perhaps music could open a door now, could hand over the key to unlock the vault. Not the vault I keep locked against lovers and friends, but the lock against myself. The vault that hides my softer heart, the one that was there before I felt the world betrayed me, before I grew distrustful: "You can't trust anyone" and "people leave." The one that harbors, protects, and safe-keeps that innocent child, the one who walked to synagogue, holding my father's hand, and all was right with the world.

Yes, maybe music could open doors in the way that dancing to the Dead liberated me, in the way that listening to the Women's Music Collective supports me, mirrors my reality, helps me to feel known and seen. Music, creaking open the rusted door, the way that classical music could bring me to tears with the ache of a clarinet, the soul shifting of a cello, the cry of the viola. With music I might find words.

I flip through the few records I packed: *Blue* by Joni Mitchell, *Giant Step* by Taj Mahal, *American Beauty* by Grateful Dead. I threw in a few jazz albums at the last minute: Cannonball Adderley, McCoy Tyner, and Bill Evans.

I turn on Cha's old record player, open the plastic lid of the dusty turntable, blow hard on the needle.

How many nights had a line from a song or a piano solo's meanderings inspired the first line of a poem? Maybe, just maybe…

I slip Cannonball Adderley out of its jacket and put the needle down on "One for Daddy-O."

In Cha's comfortable chair I pull the afghan close, sit back, and close my eyes. The minor blues start out upbeat, cheerful. Adderley's alto saxophone comes in as the piano lays down the chorus. In comes Miles Davis on the trumpet, and the tune moves into a traditional call and response. Miles's riff is sparse, probing. The tune turns wistful. Hank Jones solos on piano, a sweet answer to Miles's introspection.

Art Blakey's drums are like ocean waves gently crashing in and out as the trumpet soars.

I listen, thinking: *This is my story*—a story of the New York streets, subway cars, the Lower East Side, crowds of people, being at my father's side, and losing him. It's not "Edward the Dyke," but it is my story. The music mirrors my grief, which includes the joy of memory, the music in the simple rhythms of daily life.

Jones's piano gently accentuates the low-key but joyful tone as the trumpet reaches for the high notes, not unlike my own reaching for words. Davis reaches for the right note to tell the listener: this is loss and yearning but infused with joy! Although my father left me, I still have Green Tara, the band, Berkeley, and poetry. There is still joy.

The vault creaks open:

Lex and 67th the corner luncheonette
I'm sipping an egg cream fizzy sweetness

Another piano riff that for the life of me sounds like walking a New York City street with the cry of a truck horn, the beautiful girls in their high heels and short skirts, the street sweeper, police sirens and people in groups and alone.

Back on that swiveling stool
Afternoon half light
On that street you're that upbeat jazz chord
The one that wraps itself around my heart

And then the piano comes back this time with the conviction: despite the sadness, the longing, life is joyful, and here for the taking.

I flip the needle back to the beginning of the tune, scribble more lines:

enveloped in your presence.
You were SO big, and talking. Always talking.
Your legacy: A love of food and strangers.

For is this not where the fire lives? In a memory of a perfect moment, shared with a person who protects, loves, and admires me? Is this not my kernel? Is this not the true story of my father and me: that life, scary and painful as it is, is still worth living? Tell it slant, instructs Emily Dickenson. This is about as slant as I can get.

The picture of sitting in our corner luncheonette is so vivid, so alive, I can hear the newspapers rustling, the shouts of greeting, the milkshake machine whirring. Tears stream, as if just the picture of my father in my mind breaks open the kernel, lights the fire, eases the ache.

And though I know I need another stanza, a last line for each section comes through my pen:

Your headstone is a mess, Daddy-O.

* * *

WITH TREMBLING HANDS, a tear-stained face, and gargoyle hair, I leave the burning poem, the flaming words, the heat, and step out into brisk air, the gathering dusk. With one step, I leave the world of the buried, the world of darkness. My heart is simultaneously hurt and relieved, unburdened. Did Judy know that going to the fire would have an upside, that I might experience a lightness and that lightness would lead to a healing, a soul cleansing? It's unfathomable that I wouldn't still miss my father's warm hand in mine, that I wouldn't long for a different childhood or feel burdened by loss. But in this moment, life appears a bit more hopeful. The lines feel true and real.

In slippered feet, I navigate the soft path toward the edge of the Puget Sound, the cool Northwest air a wake-up call to the moment: I can talk about my father and I'm not bleeding, I'm not writhing on the floor with my guts spilled out, I'm not a bloody mess. On the page, I think I just may have captured the sweetness of our father/daughter love, the love of the protector and the protected, the elusive butterfly in the net. I've caught our joy of parallel "being;" he, content in his space with his newspaper and schmoozing, me in my world with a fizzy egg cream and comic books—but together, always together.

Douglas fir branches are as wide as the width of the cabin. Sugar pines drop cones the size of a coffee cup, thumping to the earth in a light breeze. Here, on a damp log by the water's edge, is a lonely spot, apart from the clamdiggers at the next cabin, the kayakers, and the fishermen…. The noise of Berkeley has quieted, the steady stream of activities is on hiatus.

According to Jewish writings, it takes seven generations to break the chain of pain, of despair. My mother, the child of immigrants, never knew her grandparents left behind in Russia. I'd met my paternal grandmother's mother, Bubbe, only once. Knowledge of my family goes back only to my grandparents. Who were the generations behind them? Who was my grandfather's father, stoned to death in a pogrom; who was my grandfather's father and his father before him?

My mother's mother died after her second birthday. Her father, a Russian proletariat who had escaped Stalin in 1917, had settled his little family in Brooklyn. The matchmaker of the neighborhood made Abe a shidduch: with a widow with two sons of her own. On the surface, Esther appeared a promising match. But love was not part of this equation, and the two created a sad, dysfunctional blended family. Esther, angry at having fallen down a notch, now with a working-class husband who drove a taxi instead of her deceased accountant, took her frustrations out on my mother, forcing her to polish her Shabbas silver, scrub floors, and hang laundry on the lines in the backyard. She was Cinderella to Esther's sons—the two princes. Whatever love of Judaism Esther could have engendered was killed while my mother mopped floors as the boys played.

Along the water's edge, the shells of clams and mussels pile in sharp shell mounds, the salty and dank smells of seaweed and mud omnipresent. The ferry from Vashon to Seattle drifts by, white smoke billowing from its stack.

I feel sad for my mother, but my mother is not where the fire lives. I never experienced the soul connection with my mother that I held so dear with my father. Still, like the S'Homamish to this land, there is an invisible umbilical cord, the natives to this place, me to my mother. While my father and I had our spiritual lives, our Jewish lives, and our unspoken understanding, my mother was blessed with artistry, a wildflower growing up through Brooklyn's concrete cracks. Sitting on the stoop of the old brownstone, my mother discovered that chopsticks could be employed as knitting needles, and with salvaged yarn she knitted, alone. One day, the neighborhood ladies noticed and took her in, taught her to knit properly. Knitting was a craft that would bring her joy her entire life. Her aesthetic was in everything she did, from sketching with pencils to painting with a watercolor set one of the neighbors gifted her for her tenth birthday. Her confidence at a high, at eighteen she begged her father to send her to art school. His answer? An unequivocal "no." After barely surviving the Great Depression driving a taxicab, the idea of training in anything as impractical, as frivolous, as uncertain as art was out of the question. She was silenced, sent to secretarial school.

It wasn't until she met my father that my mother found her artistic voice again. With him, she had permission to explore her creativity. My father's mother adored her. With warmth and empathy my grandmother took her in, folding her into the family and offering the mothering Jean so desperately needed.

My mother spent evenings knitting away, needles clacking while she created sweaters for her children, gifts for new babies, blankets, hats, and mittens. Knitting was one way into creativity, even if her pull toward a deeper artistry haunted her. She squirreled away drawings, renderings of her children, fruit bowls, country scenes.

Will becoming a writer now break the chain of our seven generations of despair, of abuse, of women's oppression? My grandmother and her mother running from the pogroms, their foremothers too. My motherless mother running from grief and an evil stepmother.

Arriving in Berkeley often feels fated. I have run also, but at the same time, I have arrived.

The water laps in larger swells as a second ferry enters the Sound. Will finding words for my grief break the chain?

* * *

"THE PERSONAL IS POLITICAL." I hear Robin Morgan's words in my head, those often read at our consciousness raising meetings. Is being a white girl who doesn't follow the script political? Is leaving home political?

The sun is low in the now-gray sky. Am I here now to rectify seven generations of pain? Is my generation, who has grown up in post-war abundance, the one to carry out the dreams of our mothers? Am I to become the family artist, the one to express, describe, and record?

* * *

THAT EVENING, THE STARS DUST ON A BLACK CLOTH, Cha bounds in with food and enough energy to power a building. I take a breath, willing myself to transition from solitude and tears to social.

"Just checking on you." She flips the kettle on. "How's the writing, Shakespeare?" she asks, setting up a pot of freshly brewed Assam.

"Rough." I curl into the soft chair while Cha putters. "And good," I answer slyly.

Cha hands over a cup of hot tea prepared just the way I like: a little milk and a spoonful of sugar. She pulls herself up onto the counter. "Tell. What is the 'something good?'"

"What do you think of the idea that it takes seven generations to heal a family wound?"

"I'm not sure," she answers pensively, sipping from her own cup of black tea. "I'm not sure I could trace back seven generations. Why?"

I tell her that after my grandmother's mother (just three generations) the trail is cold—I don't know my ancestors or anything about them.

"Maybe the idea is that no one can go back seven generations. That it takes a lifetime to heal old wounds," Cha posits.

I take this in. Right. How many of us can trace seven generations? Of course, that is the answer to the teaching: old wounds live on in our genetic makeup.

The two of us sit with our tea in the gloam, the woodsy symphony a lovely, comforting shawl. My nerves have stopped vibrating, and I'm finding my balance back to equilibrium.

"What was the something good?" Her eyes light up, ready for a good yarn.

I am conflicted. Would telling her now about "Daddy-O" dilute its power? Would it curse me finishing the poem? What if she judges the whole enterprise self-indulgent? Doubtful, since she has been a proponent of my work. But I'm not certain that she can meet me at this level, or relate to this practice of archeology, of searching for the fire. But isn't it exactly that doubt that stopped me from trying? It's too personal.

The personal is political. I take the plunge.

"After you left yesterday, I had the idea to listen to music, you know, as a way into the writing, into the issue I was blocked about. Usually, reading a poem or a piece by another author is enough. But then I remembered how music often inspires me to write."

"Go on." The tea steams and Cha focuses her gaze, present and open.

"So I dug out a couple of records I had packed. 'One for Daddy-O' by Cannonball Adderley jumped out. I figured, hey, if I'm supposed to write about my pain, I have to start writing about my father."

I put on the record and tell her about Judy, about her advice and her critique.

"Wow. That's harsh." She settles herself closer, sitting on a leather hassock next to my chair. "I think your work gets at a lot of kernels." She pats my knee. Cha smiles her crooked smile, a pale flush in her cheeks. "You know it's okay if you do nothing, right?

Even if you did nothing but think here in the cabin, that's fine too. It's all part of the process."

I can swear Cha is channeling Green Tara. When she closes her eyes, being in her presence is all I need; her equanimity and compassion come through the years she has spent cultivating her own compassion practice up here in the Northwest. In this moment, Cha sees me in the way I need, the vulnerable, the struggling, the searching, and the strong—the whole me.

I force a halfhearted grin. Two days left to my retreat. Maybe, just maybe, I'll finish the poem. Maybe, just maybe, I'm on the right path. I decide to wait to read her anything. I let it go for now, bending down to plant a big fat kiss on Cha's lips.

CHAPTER 25

Coast Starlight

The Coast Starlight chugs noisily out of the Seattle station, wheels screeching as they scrape metal rails, heavy cars creaking under their own weight. On the platform, a damp-eyed Cha waves. My heart, blasted open by the deep dive into my soul, the excavation of the poetic kernel, clicks, an anemone closing up shop. The world I am going back to is too cold for tenderness.

The dalliance with Cha was passionate, intense. Cha is a friend. She is light and energetic like Cloud but without Cloud's dreams of grandeur. If I was in the market for a girlfriend, she would be a front runner. But I'm not.

As the train rolls away from the endless expanse of Puget Sound, the soft "wave music" that I have come to love, mutes. I try to capture it, to hold the *slap slap slap* of small waves on the shore, of the foghorn and the ferries, but the train's engine and metal scraping on the tracks drown out all sound. We travel to the west of Mount Rainier, its pointy, snow-covered peak pointing arrowlike to heaven, a faraway magical land fit only for deer and bears, coyotes and eagles.

The train trip ahead is long—two days. I could drive, but trains intrigue me. I like handing over the reins of my life, not unlike the suspended sense in an airplane minus the anxiety of being at 30,000 feet. The history of train travel touches the romantic part of me. I fantasize about families arriving en masse to the West Coast in search of a better, new life. I love the tracks that wind snakelike through the forests far away from six lanes of traffic, cars, trucks, and all buzzing vehicles. On a train, I dip into a serene space, a place of solitude: I am alone in the world—in a good way. Alone, with a ringside seat to landscape and beauty, alone with my thoughts.

I'm heading home with a sheaf of new poems. With luck, I found a way to my kernel, to my fire. I'm grateful for music, its evocative nature, grateful for finding the key into "Daddy-O." Even if I haven't answered Judy's call completely, at least I have peeked inside the vault.

In this moment, I am satisfied. The retreat, a deep bow to the fact of poetry having claimed me after the first days of angst and struggle, was a success.

After drafting "Daddy-O," new poems flowed from the tap of words. "Daddy-O" isn't finished, but it will be soon. I won't file it or forget about it. I will go back until it sings!

The mid-July afternoon is grey and dreary, but my mood is sunny, undaunted by the pall. By evening we will be in Oregon, and by morning, Emeryville. The retreat has brought something else to light: I need a schedule, pronto. How else will these snippets, phrases, and musings be worked into real poems? As I struggle with "Daddy-O," I know that other poems will also demand patience and time. I'm not sure which activities will go and which will stay, but I trust I will find my way.

Volcanic mountains, smaller than Rainier but majestic nonetheless, are off in the western distance: Mount Jefferson and Mount Hood. The Coast Starlight rumbles along toward Eugene. The tracks are parallel with the freeway now: flatbed trucks loaded with logs whisk by, signs on the truck's side boast "Oregon Toothpicks." My heart aches for the logging that devastates the thick forests with clear cutting. The logging sites aren't visible from the train, but I know they are there, east of where the towns are, away from the critical eyes of tree huggers and environmentalists.

My head bobbing with the train's rhythm, I recount one poem that did come as a gift; it was a dream.

I'm walking in a leafy neighborhood when I see a Buddha in the garden. I take in the sighting as a sign. I would post the dream over my desk.

My meditation practice, encouraged by Mildred, has been deepening. There is no model for how a Jewish meditator lives in the world, but for now, that is a conflict to be resolved later. Berkeley offers a smorgasbord of spiritual paths: Hari Krishnas live in a temple on Oregon Street and welcome all. Every day, white-clad devotees dance and sing in the streets with their begging bowls, Zen Buddhists meditate in the *zendo* on Russell Street. There are the Taoists, renewal Jews, Christian Scientists, Theosophists, Jews for Jesus, Jews Against Israel, Aquarian Minyan for hippie Jews, Conservative and Orthodox temples, as well as traditional Protestant, Lutheran, Catholic, and Baptist churches scattered around town.

Unaffiliated, for now, my temples are my walks through the redwood, bay, and oak forests, listening to creeks and rivers and in the grand sweep of the Sierras where I pray private prayers, prayers for change and prayers for peace.

* * *

AFTER A NIGHT OF LIGHT, RESTLESS SLEEP, my mood sours. Today is July 19th, the anniversary of my father's death.

"Your headstone is a mess, Daddy-O," I copy and then scribble a few new lines on my yellow pad. I wish I were home now, not on a moving train, still some three hundred miles from the falling-down house. What was entertaining yesterday becomes tiring today; out of the Cascade range and the Shasta region, the landscape offers only dry brown hills. My back aches, and I feel grimy and tired.

Guilt. Are these the last lines? I have not visited his gravesite, not cleared leaves, not placed the rock at the top of the large granite headstone, the Jewish ritual to indicate that I have visited. I am ashamed. Is that the fire?

Barren low hills of Redding, Winters, Vacaville pass in a blur. The unfinished poem gnaws. A weight descends. *July 19th.* The day of the baseball game, boys against the girls. The winning followed by the bad news. The cheers and being dropped to the depths by Irma's words: "Turn for the worse."

Tears fall from my closed eyes. In that liminal space, I stand near the open grave. All around, relatives, friends, gray sky, black, black, black. The Rabbi, my father's distant cousins, navy buddies, colleagues, all in attendance to witness the spectacle of untimely death. Of a father leaving two children and a young wife. Of a man cut down in his prime, a big man being called to heel.

A cemetery is no place for a child. No place for a small person with everything in front of her, forced to face decades fatherless. My mother keening, my grandmother holding her. The horror of it all.

I jerk awake, wishing the morning light to erase the sad memory, the bitter tableau.

I scratch out another line:

I'll always remember the night we lay in the dark
Crickets the only sounds beside our voices
As we lay in the dark

You regaled me with tales of pushing your knish cart
On Coney Island.

I scribble more words: *Cyclone roller coaster, bumper cars, stuffed toys. How could those Sunday afternoons be gone forever? What are the words for breaking?*

After the kiss, Cha and I made love. We stayed in bed that night, talking. I told her about my struggles with the "fire," how music saved me. I finally read the fragments of "Daddy-O."

"No ending yet," I apologized.

"No apologies."

By the end of the last line, Cha was quietly crying. She pulled me to her. "Why didn't you tell me?" Every ounce of her midwestern goodness spilled over me, her untethered empathy, her uncomplicated compassion, her Tara-ness.

"I don't tell anyone."

For a long time, we lay close to one another as the cabin grew dark. When Cha got up to light a fire, she pulled out a bottle of wine that had been stored below the cabinets.

"'Daddy-O' deserves a toast," she said, opening what turned out to be a sublime bottle of Petite Syrah, "and I need a drink. Joanie Pinecone—I'm breaking." She handed over a glass of wine, attending to the wood stove. "I knew you had a soft side, but I didn't know how fragile you are. What a loss…." Cha took my head in her arms and rocked me, and to my surprise, the catch in my throat loosened, the vault creaked open, and I was on her shoulder, wracked with ineffable sadness. I hadn't cried since the funeral—who had time? My mother was in bed, smoking and eating ice cream, relatives were calling me to attend to her. There was junior high school, boyfriends, and a chance to be somebody else—new friends, new life. All of my tears, locked up in this cabin on this silent island, started as a creek and ended as a flood.

We pulled apart, Cha wiping my face with her red bandana. Lying back, wine in hand, she said, "You know that you are a great poet, right?"

I barely broke a smile. "And that all great writers have suffered terrible pain, right? You're in good company, Joanie! Sylvia Plath and Elizabeth Bishop—lost their fathers as children."

I listened, taking the information, my depleted soul crying for rest.

Cha slid out of the bed and, like a magician pulling a white rabbit out of a top hat, produced a veritable buffet of culinary surprises from her backpack: a salty, aged goat cheese, sweet dried apricots, smoked almonds, and Japanese rice crackers. She proudly set the feast on the table and invited me over, lighting a candle.

"For 'Daddy-O.'"

"Thank you, Cha. But how did you know…what if I'd done nothing?"

"I would celebrate your nothing," Cha laughed.

We sipped the rich wine in silence, nibbled the cheese and nuts. Outside, owls, night birds, and coyotes call. In our silence, we could hear the Sound lap.

"How did your father die?"

"I was ten. He got sick. I didn't know how sick. He was in and out of the hospital for a year. After a few months, my mother suffered a terrible car accident after visiting him. My grandmother, a Polish immigrant who had retried from work as a seamstress, came to live with me and my sister. It was bad. Both my parents were in the hospital for more than six months."

My throat tightened as I remembered my grandmother's strong hands washing my long hair in the bathroom sink.

"He died. Two months before my twelfth birthday."

"Daddy-O."

"Yes."

Cha took my hand and held it. Unlike Annice, her comforting, loving touch had brought the words to the surface. I remembered my aunt sitting with me at the funeral parlor and holding my hand. Sometimes, a hand was all I needed.

The next morning Cha was up, making coffee, preparing to leave for her studio in Seattle. Two days later she would return to drive me to the ferry and then to the station.

"Would you come back to read at the local bookstore?" she asked. "The owner is a friend."

I smiled for the first time in the week I'd been there. "So you're my agent now?"

"Why not? You need one."

I soaked in her joy and the invitation while she made breakfast.

"I leave you to your own devices!" Cha sang after breakfast. She took a deep, dramatic suck of salty air and embraced me in a warm hug.

My last day in the cabin I sketched out three more poems. Clearly, "Daddy-O" had been the plug in the drain, the block in the roadway, the sandbar to the ocean. Once dislodged, words flowed about Inez, about Jake, about the natives in the Bay Area, the Ohlone. I was getting closer.

* * *

I WALK TO THE RESTAURANT CAR in search of coffee and toast. The shift from joy and satisfaction to my current state of worry and fear is familiar in a discouraging way. Why is it that after a joyous time, even a breakthrough, I find myself back in a dark, familiar place of loss? Is this the life of a poet? After the breakthrough, it's back to the salt mines?

CHAPTER 26

Sunflowers, Wild Berries, and Goatherds: The Circus Moves North

I've been back in Berkeley two weeks. "Daddy-O" is finished and published in *Woman Spirit*. I cried the first time I read "Daddy-O" at open mic night at the North Berkeley Library. I cried, but I read through the tears. The response was strong, supportive, loving. Judy wrote me a note after that read, "Congratulations on walking through the fire! I feel you!"

Jake and Debbie are at band practice, and I'm taking the day for quiet. The retreat revealed how the magnet of solitude pulled me.

"I was invited to live at Woman Space," reports Cha on our weekly phone call.

I watch the sunflowers dance in the breeze in the back garden, orange-scented air passing through the open windows of the falling-down house. Is Cha considering leaving Lorene? I don't ask.

"You would leave Vashon?" I ask, surprised and not surprised. Cha has been circling the closely knit Her Lands movement since relocating to the Northwest. A forest sprite in a woman's body, a water nymph and a witch, a healer and a midwestern version of Green Tara, Cha might be, but somehow I can't quite see her as a rutabaga farmer and goatherd.

Since the retreat and our rekindled romance, we've been flirting. Neither of us makes a definitive move, but our connection over "Daddy-O" opened a door to intimacy. Her wisdom, understanding, and compassion pull me closer.

"I don't know if I would leave Vashon. A group in Southern Oregon is looking for a few more women to join."

"When?" I ask, the words southern Oregon conjuring an expanse of green land, lazy clouds, creeks, rivers, and the smell of hay in summer and rain in winter.

The Northwest is still wild. Berkeley has been tamed. Though there are rustic parks, and open land to explore, rough and free spirits could live in Oregon cheaply and quietly. With the Cascade Range of mountains to climb and the mighty Columbia's stunning gorge, its low land prices, and the network of hippie farmers, women too want to get in on the action, out of California. The Bay Area may be the spark of change, but there are hazards in California that weigh on us. Just over the border at Telegraph and Alcatraz, the racial tension between Berkeley and Oakland is palpable. The cost of living inches up every day, the close-knit academic community opens their doors but only so wide. Outside of the Bay Area, racism is alive and well, and, although we don't speak of it, we women, we lesbians, are as ghettoized to live in Berkeley as the Jews in Venice. Take a Barbara Hammer film to Walnut Creek? I don't think so. Get the band a gig in Sacramento? Nope.

Cha tells me that for her to move to Oregon, she would have to come up with $3,000. She has it, but she isn't sure that she wants to part with it just yet. And Her Lands requires a five-year commitment.

"Five years," I repeat. I'm trying to wrest myself out of my own fantasy of living on the land. "What about your research?" Cha was entranced with and studying the S'Homamish. "We can't forget them," she told me when she decided to commit to a Ph.D. program at Washington State.

"I could work there, do my research in Eugene, and work on the land. It's forty acres outside, just outside of Eugene. The plan is to raise goats and chickens, make cheese, garden. The land is hospitable. Oh, and it has a rushing creek with swimming holes and even a little beach area."

I put myself in Cha's position, weighing the beauty and the tedium. Living near a running creek, building a life, and engaging in shared purpose with a community of like-minded women are temptations, seductions, with isolation as the price of admission. "What about Lorene?"

"Lorene would be an issue. She needs to be in Seattle for her teaching job. As to friends, we would be twelve women on this land and there are other parcels owned by women in the area. I'd have a lot to learn. Some of the women know about tractors and machine maintenance, fence building and carpentry...."

I remembered the women enrolled in the trade classes at Laney.

Before we hang up, she throws a zinger: "Are you interested?"

Ah. Cha is making the move I thought that neither of us would make. To my surprise, my first response was not a flat "No." In the moment she asked, I wonder: *Could this be my opportunity to live alone? Could I live on the land, as Cha's lover, in my own cabin, and write? I have some money stashed away—but what about the city? What about school?* I was taken aback and at the same time thought, *This could be a chance to investigate, or at least to live out one fantasy.* I thought, *I'm still young. School can wait.*

"Intriguing, but...I'm not sure," I answer.

"Think about it," Cha sings, cheerfully signing off.

Just a year ago I considered joining Thea and Rosalie on their move to Southern Oregon. The twenty-acre parcel of land adjacent to the beautiful land where we frolicked at the Woman Spirit festival was available. In the end I abandoned the idea. Now, I'm in a conundrum; while nature is the balm to my aching soul, the city feeds my mind. In that boxing match, my mind wins. I need to learn, to meet people, to be stimulated, to grow. Picking berries, planting lettuce, and tending goats is a noble calling, just not for me. The pulse of the city is in my blood, like the wail of a jazz saxophone. For now, at least, Berkeley is the perfect balance point between the hustle of New York and the solitude of Vashon Island.

But there is Cha. And "self-sufficiency" is on everyone's lips. It is the next step in our revolution. "Not working for the man" and living off the grid. Grow our own food, make our own bread, independent and apart.

From where I sit, there is effecting change by protesting and there is effecting change by disappearing and being self-sufficient off the grid and out of the rat race. Both are empowering, but at this moment, I am invested in the changing of laws, the building of support systems for abused women, facing down racism, sexism, and ableism and changing the rules.

"The personal is political" loops, loops, and loops again.

CHAPTER 27

Ladders to Nowhere and the God Cult

It's one of those perfect Bay Area days that inspires gratitude, joy, and wonder: How did I get so lucky? The sky is cloudless, the sun warm but not hot, the temperature hovering at a mild sixty-eight degrees, the air fresh with ocean and bay, salt, and sand. Even the mudflats' uplifting driftwood sculptures, found art, and silliness spread out against the backdrop of the bay like a fine art gallery. Views stretch west to Mount Tamalpais, the bay opening out to the ocean past the Golden Gate, and east, the Bay Bridge, that workhorse erector set of a construction project, leads out of Berkeley and into the magic of the city. I am driving to school when "our song" comes on the radio.

"Because two hearts are two hearts and two minds are two minds, you...ooh oooohh."

Jake asked to take my poem "Strong and Free" and write music. She played it for her new band. They agreed to record it for their first album. Here it is being played on the local jazz station!

I am awed as Jake's voice and drums and the band's instruments blast from the radio. My words reaching out, out to people I don't know, out.

Berkeley is culture. It is films, art, painting, sculpture, and plays. It is the Grateful Dead, Country Joe and the Fish; there are the Crusaders; Earth, Wind & Fire; rock and roll; folk music; the blues; Indian music; Balinese music from Nonesuch; and what is emerging as "new age" music from Windham Hill: the spacey meditations of George Winston, Darol Anger, and Barbara Higbie.

It is beat poetry, women's confessional poetry, language poetry, and rants. It is collage, painting, photography.

And it is nature: rose gardens and bottle brush, Japanese irises and birds of paradise grow from the cracks in the sidewalk, in dry patches of earth, in abandoned lots. It is wild with trees: Norfolk pines, palm trees, redwoods, oaks, and bay laurels. It is creeks and the bay and even the occasional lake. Life is electric; there is always some cool event, a reading, a performance, a concert, an opening.

But how is one to survive? How to enjoy the bay's cornucopia of culture and politics while living in a clean apartment and writing poetry? When I examine the lives of women writers—Colette, Woolf, Cather—I understand that their finances were taken care of, some by men, others by family money, but all secure. Recent writers manage to write while working: Toni Morrison, Alice Walker. Writing while working is a better option than not writing.

So that is my question: How do women navigate the art world without financial support? One thing is obvious: work paths need an overhaul, a reinvention, a reimagining. To ensure funding many women apply for grants—a mysterious, competitive, and labyrinthine world—or go into teaching, a traditional path that pays about as well as any other pink-collar job: nurse, caregiver. Of course, many women, feminist or not, take the path of least resistance, suffering under the mantle of labor—counter and waitstaff work in cafés, gardening, bookstore staff, librarian. Anything to continue to feed the mind, even if the creative work is relegated to "the side." The important issue is to assure that schedules were flexible, to allow us to be at the ready for the next political emergency, the next festival, the next gig.

But after limping along financially, we as a community are feeling the strain. The political atmosphere is pointing toward a new conservatism, grants drying up, the ride on the welfare train ending. What is next? A few select doors open while some remain shuttered. Food service jobs are abundant as Berkeley boasts a disproportional number of restaurants and bars to residents. But restaurants are a ladder to nowhere. I try but can't shake the traditional path of working for a living! In the end, I am not willing to suffer the life of impoverished poet. I was finished with the falling down house, scraping for food and money. I want both the artistic life and a few creature comforts. So....

One traditional path, one many have chosen, is to go into business by starting at the bottom as a white man's secretary, succumbing to subservience. Out of the question. Skirts? Stockings? Pumps? I don't think so. Besides, how far could one climb, really? The glass ceiling is locked into place. I might start as a secretary but would be lucky to be promoted. What sets me apart is that I don't mind wearing the skirts, or even the shoes: it is the serving and, worse, the boredom of the available industries in San Francisco. Mind-numbing jobs are abundant in banking, real estate, the telephone company, advertising.

The truth is, short of being a doctor, lawyer, banker, or accountant, job opportunities are slim.

"You will be a leader," the astrologer tells me as my turn comes for a private audience with Cha's trusted psychic and seer. In a ramshackle neighborhood of southwest Seattle, Cha found Deborah through Lorene, who knew the psychic. How they raved about her!

Deborah's house is a small, claustrophobic concoction of what I called "spiritual detritus." Kwan Yin, Buddha, candles, tables cluttered with crystals and tarot cards. Deborah is a lumbering, heavy-set woman, a little bedraggled, the antithesis of a clear-headed "seer." We arrive in Cha's battered station wagon, the last appointment before I board my train for the Bay Area in the fall. Deborah welcomes us, offers tea, and reads our charts.

"A leader?" At that moment I can barely lead myself from home to school and back again without stopping to write a poem, or an idea for one.

"Four planets are clustered around your mid-heaven, on the cusp between the ninth and the tenth house. Those houses represent career. All are in Scorpio: Moon, Venus, Mars, and Mercury. There is no question about it, Joanie, you will lead." Deborah looks up at me more directly for the first time. "You will know when the opportunity presents itself, or, I should say, it will find you."

"And here?" She points to the sun positioned in the eighth house. "That's the death of your father? When did you lose him?" she asks, her face expressionless.

* * *

LEADING. OK. BUT FIRST, GETTING STARTED! Hard work is in my blood. My parents, children of immigrants, were hard workers, always pushing and taking risks. Beside the financial benefits, they both craved the sense of purpose of work as much as they needed air.

Cloud moved to an ashram in southern California. I was sad to see my friend and mentor leave town, no return date. Like Cloud, is being a nun, a monk, an acolyte, the answer to the poet and artist's money dilemma? It was Cloud's alternative. Not only am I vehemently not interested in being anyone's follower, the life of an ascetic isn't a match. I am all sharp edges—a porcupine—quills up, ready to spray the next interloper. I could never fit myself into a regimented lifestyle. Yes, I appreciated the benefits of cultivating inner peace, but monastic life has zero pull. After her move, I realized I hadn't known Cloud at all. How could a spirit as joyful and free as hers fold herself into a box and adhere to the rigors of monastic life?

I try compartmentalizing, keeping the question of money, finances, and career at arm's length. I stay busy writing, going to school, and working at a bookstore. All the while the question dogged me: *What next? How to earn a living?*

CHAPTER **28**

Coney Island Sunday (1962)

We don't mean to stay out all day, but after picking up rent checks, Daddy drives in the opposite direction of home. Once in a while, on a grey Sunday, when mom hankers for a kasha knish, or when Daddy is feeling nostalgic, we load into the large Pontiac to drive to Coney Island, but never alone.

I can count the times I have been alone with my father on one hand. OK, maybe two. Picking up bagels on Sunday mornings. Walking to the corner for a newspaper and an egg cream at the luncheonette. Picking up dry cleaning on Queens Boulevard on Saturday afternoon. In Brooklyn, there are Saturday afternoon walks to the manicurist, the woman who keeps his nails trim and clean, with a stop at the old newsstand for a *MAD* magazine and comic books.

But this isn't an errand. It isn't a half hour. It isn't an obligation. This is a full day, a Sunday. Mom is home. Would she mind? Spring has just burst in New York. May. The sun is high and warm but not hot and not a drop of the humidity that will descend on the city in June.

Daddy parks the big Pontiac and heads straight to Nathan's Famous. A hot dog and thick French fries for me, potato knish and a burger for him. "I sold knishes on the beach here," Daddy points west to the wide sandy beach. "With Uncle Joe. The knish place gave us a cart. We'd push that heavy cart up and down the beach yelling, 'Hot knishes! Hot dogs! Hot knishes! Ten cents! Get your hot knishes!' We lived just over there...." He points east to the rows of dark brick brownstones.

"Did you sell many?"

"Many? We sold out every time! The sun and the beach make people so hungry! Even if they'd brought a little sandwich, after a swim and walking on the beach they were famished."

"Was it fun living at the beach?"

The idea of being able to swim all summer without driving to a beach seems like a dream.

"In a way. Summer was great, but the winters were rough. The winds blew off the ocean icy and damp. In the summer, the crowds would pour off the subways like lemmings. But Grandma loved the sun. Sending us kids to the beach was the best babysitter she could have."

I cannot picture my old buxom Nana lounging on her porch on a Sunday afternoon, face turned toward the sun. Nana is always on the move, her gray hair tied up in a braid circling her skull. All week she and Papa Harry labor as tailors. I know from listening to my parents talk that the unions fight for worker rights, shorter hours, better conditions that never seem to materialize. All day she sits bent over a whirring sewing machine. At night she is exhausted from raising three children and from a loveless arranged marriage.

After Nathan's, our bellies warm and full, we wander the board-walk, sipping our drinks—Dr. Brown's Cream Soda for me, seltzer for Daddy. The merry-go-round's festive calliope is counterpointed by roller coaster riders' screams as the rickety cars descend the steep decline of the Cyclone. There is no need to ask: I am neither brave enough, old enough, or tall enough to ride what is billed as the "biggest roller coaster in New York City."

What I am after are the bumper cars. Daddy pays for a ticket and I slip behind the wheel, bumping cars with other maniacal kids who are counting the days until they are handed the keys to a V-8 Chrysler or Cutlass Supreme. I ride, bumping out frustrations I don't even know I had! Frustration living in a three-room apartment, sharing a room with my sister, frustration with school and teachers and kids who aren't yet up to reading chapter books or calculating simple math equations because my parents have turned down the second-grade teacher's offer for me to skip a grade. I want to soar, I want to read *Nancy Drew* and discuss her capers, how she unravels mysteries! Adrenaline pumps, waking up my revenge with every surprise bump from behind or side. The huge hall echoes with childish screams.

Ears ringing from the dizzying crash of bumper cars and kids screaming, Daddy and I go back to strolling the boardwalk. Past the spinning teacups, the mini roller coaster for little kids, and the splash pool are the arcade games, rows of hawkers trolling for paying customers. Throwing a few coins on the counter for the ring toss, Daddy picks up a metal ring. No luck.

Next to the ring toss is the water gun game. With a hard stream of water, players aim for the mouth of a clown. When enough water fills the hole, a balloon expands over the clown's head. Keep the water coming and the balloon pops. That's a winner! I stand by in wonder: Daddy with a gun? He looks like a natural.

Blam! Blam! Blam! Each spray of water shot out of the gun hits the clown's mouth smack in the center.

I jump up and down. I am not just jumping because Daddy is winning, I am jumping because Daddy is playing!

All we ever see of Daddy is Daddy dragging in from work, tired. Daddy eating, Daddy on the phone, Daddy yelling! But Daddy playing? It is a wonder, an anomaly, another world.

The wrinkled, gray attendant with the half-soaked apron asks, "Which prize, Mister?" He points at the teddy bear on the shelf, the ballerina doll, and the goldfish swimming in a tank.

"Goldfish," he says, as if he has this all planned.

The attendant scoops a goldfish out of the tank and with one swift movement fills a plastic bag with fish and water. Daddy hands it over to me.

I stare at the small orange fish, entranced by its orange body and angelic fins, its tiny mouth opening and closing, opening and closing.

Daddy laughs. "I never even had a pet fish!"

"But you had a knish!"

He pats my head at the silly rhyme and the memory of pushing his cart with his little brother.

We stroll past the forklift game as the sun climbs. I squint at the afternoon brightness, passing the balloon shooting game and the bag toss, mooning over my new pet. "What should we name her?"

"Winner!"

I peered into the plastic bag. "Hello, Winner!"

Daddy smiles. The smell of sugar and baking things waft toward us as we near the sweet shop.

"Cotton candy? Ice cream?"

"Nah, I'm full of French fries."

We pass the little kids licking cones, parents wiping mouths, and teenage girls tearing tiny pieces of spun sugar off giant cotton candy puffs. We pass the Ferris wheel. Daddy knows that I don't like things that move in circles because I get dizzy and throw up so we keep walking. Daddy stops abruptly in front of the Skee-Ball lanes, my favorite game. The change in his pocket jingles—quarters, dimes, and nickels looking for a home.

"Wanna try?"

I place the plastic bag with Winner gently down. "I'll be right back," I say, and kiss the bag.

The Skee-Ball is heavier than I remember. Daddy comes up behind me, pulling my arm with the ball back a foot, guiding me. "Let go!"

I release the ball, propelling it down the lane.

The ball lands smack in the middle of the three rings! Bullseye!

"I won! I won!" I scream. I collect my prize—a poorly stitched bear with thin fur—when Daddy realizes the day has gotten away from us.

"Gotta go!" he says, car keys already in hand.

I snatch Winner up, and Daddy and I walk back hand in hand. The car is hot from sitting in the sun all afternoon, and the seat burns back of my legs.

I sit in the front with Daddy—usually Mom's seat—and we crank up soul music.

The echoes of riders' screams on the Cyclone send a chill up my spine—what if life were like that? An endless series of steep climbs, the exhilaration of the view, the plummet. Up and down, round and round. I wonder…how would you survive? Wouldn't you get weak with every plummet?

In the car ride home, I decide to hide this day in the deep recesses of my mind: a private date with Daddy, my new pet goldfish, Daddy a winner, and the bump and turn of the cars.

I don't know now that there is only a small handful of private hours with my father left in my short time remaining with him. I will protect it like I protect the small gold locket, like the books from the library. They are mine and mine alone. It is me and Daddy, out in the world, my small hand in his large one, safe, loved.

I look out the window, the Manhattan skyline fading from view as we head home. I am filled up in a different part of my body than where the knish landed, a different part of my heart than at school where I win prizes for reading the most books and writing the best book report. It's the part of me that lights up when I see Daddy. It's like that display in school where our teacher shows the different organs inside of our bodies by pressing a button. Up lights the stomach, liver, spleen, pancreas. A final button, and there is the heart with its valves and aorta, its muscle and pump. That's where I'm full.

CHAPTER 29

Men vs. Women

The crepuscular sky bleeds into a rich orange as the sun sets behind the trees. Blue lingers like the warmth of a good cocktail, midnight blue turning to indigo to purple to grey to black while the first stars dot the canopy of sky. "Ready?" Jake calls to Debbie from the kitchen.

"Wish me luck. I'm writing tonight," I say, leaning in the portal of my room. After lighting candles and incense, I stand at the doorway like one of Tara's lesser angels, her bodhisattvas. I've meditated, purified myself to receive.

"Good luck!" Jake sings, shooting her hand up in a high five and proffering a warm hug. "Whew!" she says, hit by a wall of sandalwood. "Write me another tune!"

I turn back to my desk but not before catching sight of her tiny butt in tight jeans disappearing down our funky hallway stippled with cracks, an uneven, unfinished wood floor, and a ragged lightbulb hanging from a cord. Guitar riffs follow her down the hall. Debbie, practicing. Jake reaches her hand into her open doorway, the music silences. In a flash, Debbie bounds out in a brown plaid flannel shirt with the tail hanging out, baggy jeans and work boots. She is ready for what will turn out to be one of her final date nights with Jake.

Tonight is my night home alone. After the retreat in Vashon, solitude is a commodity that I can't quite get enough of. I find myself longing for those long, empty days, the quiet time to listen to music and write without a time limit.

Having a few hours of assured quiet is a relief, a still pond to dip into. I am trying to keep the writing juice flowing and setting boundaries on who, what, where, and how I commit myself. Poetry has gotten locked in a struggle with real life; the writing demands not only time to scribble snippets, but dream time, blank time, even boring, empty time!

Along with the demands and obligations of our parallel careers, emotional and financial drama are taking their toll. The shuttering of Loaves and Dishes has sent us scurrying in different directions looking for work. Jake is moving in with Lynn and is experimenting with playing in two bands while band meetings, practices, and gigs have collided.

Peggy is campaigning, lobbying hard for Jake to defect to her band, Be Be K'Roche. There is Jake with a crush on Peggy. Ever the romantic, Jake falls in love about as often as I do!

My distractions include school obligations and trying to heal the relationship with my mother. On top of it all, there is the wider world: police station bombings, rumors of the FBI infiltrating women's meetings, and the Maoist study groups.

All day I've been thinking about a new poem I want to sketch out a few lines for. I am calling it "The Power of Sound." I want to capture the scene up in the Cascades with Cha where we backpacked and spent two days swimming in mountain lakes. Tonight, I have an idea to get the words flowing. In past months, thanks to a local innovative radio station, I have fallen madly in love with classical music.

Men vs. Women

I listen on a small portable radio in my room. My practice of deep listening started in the basement jazz clubs in New York where we sipped wine and listened with all the serious attention. We would give a symphony; we listened as the band leader laid down a theme, the soloists riffing. I remember one concert with Bill Evans, his long fingers flying up and down the keyboard, his unique sound of bebop, classic jazz riffs, and the blues bursting through the hammers and strings.

My love of classical music started on a field trip to see Itzhak Perlman perform at Lincoln Center. The master violinist, whom I studied in music appreciation, demonstrated what Bolero and Rimsky-Korsakov sounded like when played live. In tenth grade, I savored the wide emotional range of the violin, piano, cellos, and wind instruments, the interplay of sounds, and how the disparate piece resolved in the crescendo. But it was high school, and the coolness factor demanded my focus on rock and roll with a jazz addiction on the side. I wasn't convinced that classical music was cool enough until I heard the "music of the spheres" in Berkeley: Mozart, Beethoven, and Schumann. Now, I have grown a private passion. I say private because the women's community is not amenable to male composers.

I love piano concertos, music that captures nuances of mood. Rock and roll feeds the place in me that vibrates with anger and excitement; jazz is my sad/not sad companion. Classical captures, dare I say, my spiritual life and yearnings, connects me back to that place in the synagogue, the place of spiritual frisson, that place of God.

I reach for a pad and pen.

Moon child/water woman
Send some spray my way

I'm writing the next lines in a shape, a poetic form called a concrete poem, even though I don't know its name. The poem looks like a waterfall. I'm searching for the next line when a knock at the door breaks my concentration.

I'm alone in a loosely secured house, in south Berkeley. The door is locked, but it could easily be pushed in, breaking the rotten portal.

"Who is it?" I shout, hurrying down the hallway. In my right hand I clutch a hiking pole I've grabbed from the corner of my room. Its tip is razor sharp.

"Arthur."

I open the door, the annoyance of being interrupted eclipsed by feeling flattered at seeing Arthur on my front step.

"Just in the neighborhood?" I jibe him.

"You could say that."

"Come on in. Tea? Or a beer?"

"Beer."

With that, I know my night's work is over. I'm interested in Arthur. He has a sweet face and a golden halo of curls. I tell Arthur about our schedule of private nights and how auspicious his timing is, and he tells me he saw Jake and Debbie drive off.

"Oh, you're stalking me, are you?"

"No, just don't want to invade enemy territory."

I put on an Oscar Peterson album, invite him into my room.

Arthur sips his beer. I sip water and sit in my work chair, facing my desk. "The Angels of Light are going to open for the Dead," Arthur tells me. "At Stanford next week. You going?"

"I hadn't heard about it, but yes, I'd like to. Where do I get tickets?"

Arthur is a prior resident of the falling-down house, with Scott and Michael, but when his two friends went east, Arthur decided to get a room in another house.

Walking over to spy the half-exposed page on my typewriter, Arthur takes my hand, an electric volt.

The sex with Arthur is easy, like melting butter. A little flame and it happens. Tacitly, Arthur understands that he can't stay. We haven't posted signs, but it's clear: No Men Allowed.

The next day I hear from Thea that she's through with me. Turns out Jake and Debbie saw Arthur coming in and went to Derby Street and told Annice who told Thea. Not only are they upset that there was a man in the house, but also that I am not in lock step with the separatist army.

* * *

A WEEK LATER, TWO NIGHTS AFTER the Dead and Angels of Light show at Stanford, Jake, Debbie, and I drive to San Francisco on a Sunday night in Debbie's 1940s truck. Jake drives. Tonight, Debbie has top billing. The invitation from the women-only Full Moon Café is a perfect opportunity to road-test tunes and new lyrics. "They wanted the band, but the café is not zoned for amplified music," Debbie explains, almost apologetically. Jake is happy to take a back seat, at least for tonight. Not everyone, including Debbie, is aware how hotly she is being pursued by Be Be K'roche—and, Jewish woman that she is, guilt has been dragging her down. "I love them," she says of the Berkeley Women's Music Collective on our Strawberry Canyon walk. "But I might have a better chance with Be Be K'Roche." I advise her to try it with Peggy and the band, to try playing with both bands before making any irreversible decisions. "And, ask your dreams," I tell her. "Before you go to bed, ask your subconscious what it wants."

After finagling, we park the huge truck and walk through the fog-laced Castro streets. Eighteenth Street is the artery that is home to the gay community and particularly to the domestically-minded gay men who set up house in a neighborhood with like-minded neighbors.

Walking down Eighteenth Street, turning the corner on Douglass to the café, I make room for Debbie and Jake to walk side by side. Pulling the scarf around my neck closer, I hug my arms around the vintage leather bomber jacker I unearthed at the Alameda flea market for ten dollars. Just steps away from the café, I fend off tears, a lump in my throat. My heart is hurting and a sadness lingers on a dark, offshore fog bank. My balance, albeit a delicate one, after months of Mildred's healing, herbs, eating beets and brown rice, writing, giving readings, and growing as a poet, is about to tip into my pre-Berkeley confusion and miasma—after thinking I was on solid ground, I'm lost. In my enthusiasm about everything Berkeley, I haven't antici-pated being catapulted backward. In the last days, life has been that Coney Island Cyclone, that intimidating and terrifying rollercoaster ride of ecstasy and pain, of discovery and smackdown, of expansion and contraction.

I'm working out a lashing, being judged and criticized by friends and lovers for sleeping with Arthur, for standing my bisexual ground and excommunication by Thea. Last week, I skipped women's night for the second week. When she got home after a night out, Jake let slip that Thea has been gossiping about me around the fireplace at the White Horse. "Sleeping with men!" she announced indignantly. Who gave her proprietary rights? I have slept with Thea exactly twice. Thea's passion is the Oregon "wimmin's" land movement. Annice, having found a more emotionally available lover in Kate, isn't indignant, but she helped stoke the inflammatory conversation that, apparently, took a nasty turn when people encouraged Jake and Debbie to institute a "no men in the house" policy.

Jake broached the idea. To her credit, she talked to me alone. I balked and she backed down. After all, she has a brother. But our altercation hurt me, and I was feeling betrayed.

The smackdown was a reality check. I can go far, but how far?

Men vs. Women

* * *

THE FULL MOON CAFÉ IS WARM, low lit, and abuzz when we arrive. It's a small space on the bottom of three-story Victorian, and the owners know Debbie from Portland. It's a plum gig for Debbie, who hasn't as yet been invited to solo in the Bay Area.

While Debbie runs a sound check with the café's engineer, Jake and I order beers and settle ourselves in the middle of the audience. The lights go down. After a short introduction, Debbie launches into her set with "The Bloods." Her voice is strong, her playing on the beat.

As Debbie announces the last song of her rabble-rousing set, a blast of cold air chills the room as the front door opens with a bang. A large man, disheveled, in a light jacket and jeans barges into the café. The hair on my neck stands up. Without thinking, I grab Jake's hand.

"You bitches! You stole my wife!"

I feel like I've been punched in the stomach. Beth, the owner of the café, who has just greeted us so warmly, rushes from the back of the room.

"No men allowed here!" she shouts.

The room falls into stunned silence.

"You dykes! You awful people! Is she here?"

He barrels through the room when a clutch of large dykes wheel him around.

"Get your hands off me, you scum," he shouts, shaking his shoulders loose of pushing hands.

I'm glued to my chair in the middle of the room as women shout, "Get out," "We don't know your wife!" and "Scumbag!"

Suddenly, the bruiser spins, raising his right arm. His hand is balled into a fist.

One of the women shoots her arm into a slug, missing his jaw but landing hard on his shoulder.

A trapped animal, he swings his arms wildly. When the door opens again, two fit San Francisco patrolmen are there. With one swift move they grab his hands and, with the dykes holding him steady, cuff him.

"They slugged me!" he shouts at the cops, who hustle him out the door.

"Tell it to the judge!" one woman shouts.

Another yells, "Yeah your wife is here, but she's hiding!"

As the crowd breaks into cheers, another shouts, "If you'd treated her right, maybe she would have stayed home!"

The taunting provokes his vitriol. "You bitches. I'll get you. My kids don't have their mother. You can fuck each other till you die for all I care! But I'm getting my wife home!"

The wooden door slams behind the patrolmen and the perp. Finally, the melee is over.

Beth shouts, "Beers on the house!"

One woman locks the door as another hops on stage. Debbie, suddenly paralyzed in the stage lights, doesn't move until Jake waves her over.

"Women!" she starts.

"This is a revolution. Revolutions hurt people."

On the sidelines, Beth and Debbie nod enthusiastic approval.

The room falls silent. "That guy is a dick, yeah, but he is a casualty. There are going to be casualties. Get used to it…."

Murmurs of approval from the audience.

"When men give us our rights—to protect our bodies from rape and domestic abuse—when they give us equal pay for equal work, when we walk into the top echelons of government, when they respect our Black, brown, and Asian sisters, maybe then we'll back down. Till then, people will get hurt."

A loud, frightening knock disrupts the speaker's soapbox speech. Someone opens the door and in blow two more cops.

"I need a statement," one says calmly to Beth, who is downing a beer with shaking hands. A clutch of women huddle around her, patting her back and murmuring, "It's okay, we've got you."

Debbie's set clearly over, we pull our jackets on and trudge, sobered and shaken, back to the truck.

"You were great." Jake pats her arm. "Everyone loved it."

Debbie looks about to break into tears, but Jake's comforting voice brings her back to the cool night. For myself, again walking behind, I know what I need to do next.

CHAPTER 30

It's Over

This story began so many years ago. 1965 in Woodridge, New York. Girls against the boys. It was ten years ago, but that innocent softball game is ten lifetimes past. Sadly, here we are, still fighting. Men versus women.

Sports is just one arena where we are still fighting for our rightful place. In 1973, as we were demonstrating in Berkeley, Billie Jean King challenged Bobby Riggs to the tennis match of a lifetime. Billie Jean risked her reputation, money, and fame to prove that women were strong, determined, competitive, and aggressive. She stunned the world by beating the top-ranked tennis star, claiming her place not only for herself but for all of us.

Still, in the workplace, in jurisprudence and in the home, women remain disempowered. In 1975, women are still denied credit cards or mortgages. Glass ceilings and locked doors prevail in academia and business. Men's money, backroom dealings, and corporations still wield unjust power over women.

The battle between men and women is, beside racism, the pivotal struggle of the American century. Would American women be fighting for our rights, fighting to be restored to our rightful power, for respect, for equality, for the remainder of time? It looks like it.

How have we lost our power anyway? Witch hunts? Violence? The fear of women's power ended in destruction, insidious cruelty, and intimidated women. Men's violence against women has been perpetrated over centuries.

What happened to Cha's matriarchal societies, to women rulers, to queens? What happened to the time when women were esteemed, held up, and revered for their equanimity, meting out justice? The world's modernization and industrialization relegated women to the domestic, to repetitive tasks, away from the strategic and into the world of childbearing and child raising. We were infantilized, our mental health compromised. We became useful either as decoration or slaves. But we wouldn't be held. Come the nineteenth century, Suffragists defied the limits of those small lives; they knew that women could be so much more. And so we fight on.

That sunny summer Catskill day, the day I helped the girls beat the boys, that day filled with joy and excitement, could have gone so many ways. A pop fly could have been caught by Billie—a hard stop, a quick throw, controlled by the boys, and not the one that slipped passed him to the far outfield. Or Alan could have tagged me out at first or second base. But to hit the ball so deep into the outfield that it sailed past all the boys, liberating the girls on base to run home—that was, as we say, a game-changer. That was epic. Had it been later… maybe my grand slam would have had an impact beyond the campers at Highland Park.

The separatism is bringing me to the realization that the Berkeley chapter of my life is over. The fun, the parties, the jam sessions, the flirting, the headiness of being "on the rise." Nothing is permanent, right? So why have I allowed myself to believe that our special stretch of time will last? Aren't spontaneity and delight the stuff of magic? The magician's sleight of hand, the "now you see it, now you don't," the here and then gone, a wisp of smoke and…poof!

If anyone knows about impermanence, it is me. My father gone in a flash. In a year's time we morphed from intact family to grieving train wreck. There is nothing constant except for change.

The lingering question I ask myself, after the Full Moon Café, after the gossip and the frustration, is why do I wish and hope that things will last? Why do I hold on? Everything changes—that is how we avoid stasis. It is how we grow.

* * *

AFTER JAKE MOVED OUT TO LIVE WITH LYNN, after she left the band to join Be Be K'Roche, I took one last acid trip. It was terrible: fraught with anxiety, paranoia—a terrible case of the heebie-jeebies. We thought it would be fun. A friend and I decided to spend the afternoon in Redwood Park where, amongst a stand of first-growth redwoods, we would commune with nature. It would be like the Spring Picnic: kick back, listen to the bees buzz and the birds sing.

Without notice, my mind began to betray me—badly. Instead of doors opening to beautiful, rich insights and abounding love, my thoughts blasted open a house of horrors.

In the past, experiencing stunning insights about impermanence, basking in the infinite glory and beauty of the natural world, watching as the doors of perception opened to reveal endless creative possibilities, of magically getting a chance to do my life over, of music that spoke volumes without words, had made the risk of LSD worthwhile.

Instead, that Saturday afternoon in Redwood Park, a wide swath of green belt situated on 1,800 acres about a mile above East Oakland, I was caught, my mind snagging a thread of which I couldn't find the end, spinning violently around and around on a hamster wheel of circular thinking that could easily have been the death of me.

And a hamster wheel it was, with all the stink of a nasty cage, the dry grit of sawdust laced with pee, garbage, and other animal garbage: for the entire afternoon and the evening that followed, the questions harangued.

Why are there gorgeous stately redwoods in a park adjacent to a drug-infested city where nefarious hymns whispers underneath green fronds?

What is poetry?

What is it good for?

Why am I here?

Why bother with all the hard work of writing?

Around and around, the same questions, building a noose of stress that threatened to strangle me. I got the creeps, my skin crawling, as if every needle shot executed here was piercing me. I could hear the screams of every rape; I was in a war zone, feeling all the pain of the world: the battles, the power grabs, the poverty.

The questions flew faster, racecars on a racetrack.

Why do some kisses feel so good, so life-changing, so authentic and exciting, and others leave me cold?

Why do some lovers draw me in and others leave me as chilled as cold sorbet?

Why do I like both men and women?

Why do people like me anyway?

Why did my mother not pull the emergency brake on the steep slope of the garage?

What is family, and why do people invest so much to keep it afloat?

Why do some families last and some fall apart?

I know, I know. I tried to make sense of it all. Relationships are about interdependencies and reliability, about "being there" for the people you love. Sadly, love had dealt me more than I could handle— so much that I couldn't make sense of it! Interdependence? I didn't want to depend on anyone! Loss had left me distrustful.

Here, in Berkeley, in 1975, change and revolution were more important. I had no use for dependencies, not now! Life was calling. I didn't want to be held back, held accountable, held. I belonged to no one and no one belonged to me and that was the way I wanted it.

The questions grew darker, storm clouds over a glowing horizon.

What is my place anyway?

Am I here for a reason?

What do kudos matter, a song on the radio? A publication?

Nothing mattered. It wasn't that I was looking to exit life, I just didn't understand *why* I was working so hard, so heads-down, so driven. I was bombarded by these questions that Saturday in Redwood Park, and into that evening.

* * *

So how does the Berkeley Revolution end?

First, the government squelches, co-opts, arrests, and intimidates the left's leadership.

For us women, it is over because we have become dispirited. The infighting wears us down. We are factionalized.

For me, it ends on a personal level. It ends because I have changed. I am resistant to the separatists, to becoming a rule follower of yet another dogma, another oppressive, powerful force. And, I have outgrown the falling-down house. I want a real bed, a house without leaks, a heating system, and, yes, maybe a house with a coat of paint!

But even beyond the material, it is over for me because I crave distance from the intensity, from the comings and goings, from uncertainty. I need a plan to separate from Debbie's broken heart and band practice and house meetings. Since my ruinous time with Joy, I have promised myself that if I was ever again asked to tolerate another human's mercurial moods, idiosyncrasies, and craziness, I was going to be sleeping with them. I was finished with roommates.

I need to bring myself back into a benign state, a state that will reset my nervous system and worldview, a reset that will allow me the time and permission to make decisions for myself and write poems. I need to leave to find out who I love and how I want to love. Am I still willing to take risks, to live life as a big experiment? I am not sure.

Not the least of why "it's over" is that I need to figure out how I can continue to be a change agent without becoming a separatist.

In a way, for me, it is a graduation. I have entered a rogue school with high standards: Listen. Absorb. Process. Analyze. My course in San Francisco poetry has been my thesis. Tramping through North Beach, Berkeley, hanging around in cafés, bars, and bookstores has been a history lesson, a humanities lesson, and a sociology lesson. Workshops, publishing, editing, open mics are my work study. Listening. Absorbing. Processing. Analyzing.

I have engaged in a crash course—a community university—stepping out into the larger world, being valued.

And, I tried to save the world, I really did. I rallied for Inez; I protested against domestic abuse, capitalist greed, wars.

Now, I need to bring the war home to resolve my own battles, to rub salve on my own losses. My task demands time to parse what it means to be a woman who, at least the way it looks now, is going to be making her way on her own.

Hanging out with the band is a happy place for me. I love every one of them for their respective talents and quirks. I love their laughter.

And, I am aware that I am loving them at one of the pinnacles of their lives. We all are in the throes of becoming self-realized for the first time, at the height of Maslow's pyramid.

But I want to be my own person, not in the shadow of the band. I want my voice added to the chorus of voices that was poetry's choir. I might not know what the purpose of poetry was or where it is going or how I am going to exist as a poet, but I do know that when I hear great poetry, I am transformed. The seas part with a life-changing revelation, the unknown becomes known. It is the light of literature and words and meaning that I love best. I hope to be that agent of change for others, the one that transforms something, the words that loosen the grip of others' conundrums.

It is over for all these reasons. And the last years have taken their toll. I am weary.

That night, the acid trip relentlessly powering on, I called Jake. I don't usually ask for help or support, but Jake has been my mentor, my big sister, and wise friend. Jake, my partner in crime.

"I think I'm losing it."

Maybe it was her own run ins with drugs that triggered a fear in her, but Jake was there in a flash.

"Why?" I asked.

"Why what?"

"Why write, why here, why us?"

Jake sat with me on the porch of the falling-down house, yellow streetlights the only light source as we sat on two overstuffed chairs with the stuffing falling out. She handed me a sandwich she'd thrown together. Whole wheat bread with hummus and tomatoes, sprouts, and a few sprigs of cilantro.

"Love," Jake answered, not a hint of doubt in her voice.

"Love."

"Yes. It's all for love."

The hamster wheel slowed, the storm clouds eased back. How rarely I'd known real love. Sad memories flood: my sister and I fighting because she was planning to run away, my father screaming at my sister on the telephone when he thought she should be doing homework, my mother smoking cigarettes, off in a world of her own. The rageful impatience of my parents when my sister couldn't learn to read. Humiliations, criticisms.

Love? I remembered my father and our happy day at Coney Island.

Love who? The parents who die?

"I don't trust love."

"I understand. But I stand my ground. Love..." Jake repeated.

"I'm not sure I believe it."

Belief or no, Jake's words were calming.

The questions were still there, but they were not as urgent. I sucked hard at my water bottle, hoping to flush the drugs out of my system.

"Think about it. The band, the protests, even the bombings and the kidnapping. Done for love, right? Risks taken to save the country's soul. Protests to keep hope alive. We're the hopeful ones. Poets, musicians, artists. We do it all for love."

I consider: If I cultivate love, trust, maybe my life could work. Love begs the question of being vulnerable, and isn't being vulnerable the exact thing that makes love beautiful? To care for someone in their most fragile, open state, to be able to hold a person as they opened to you?

The truth is, I will never be as vulnerable as that eleven-year-old child who believed that big daddy was there to protect all her life long. I will never be as vulnerable as I was having a mother who disappeared into a world of sadness leaving me neglected, alone.

No friendship, no lover will ever have the weight of that first, pivotal loss. Perhaps in the future, a child, a spouse of many years, a loss that could be intolerable, will hit me. But that is so many years in the future, I can't comprehend it.

No, Jake is right. I will learn to love, to trust. If my years in Berkeley have taught me anything, it is to have more compassion and empathy for the ones whose lives are a struggle every day. Haven't compassion and empathy incited me to action? To fight the fights of women but also of silenced, the abused, people with disabilities? Perhaps it is time to extend that empathy and compassion to myself. To realize and accept what I'd lost and that I had survived.

And so I am leaving. I am leaving the falling-down house, with the chaos, the creaky steps, and the random comings and goings. I want privacy, to close the door, to see whom I want, and to sleep with whom I want. I will finish school, get serious about my future.

I am leaving to complete my self-directed thesis. To listen. To process. To regain solitude. To explore my spirituality. I am still not speaking about my father, except to Cha and Mildred—and that was through the words of "Daddy-O" with Cha, and only briefly with Mildred.

Finding the words to describe my father in a poem was a start, a toe in the water, a beginning. Now, I need to find the words to construct my own narrative: my father left, yes, but it was circumstantial not intentional. Maybe my "men leave, women are safer" story that I've told myself is misguided; I see now that we are all vulnerable when we love, when we need, when we care.

I am leaving to make a home of my own. The one bedroom that I found is over the Oakland-Berkeley line. Jake and Lynn live nearby. I'll still see my friends, the band.

The people I've met in Berkeley have changed me. The support and encouragement of Cloud, Annice, Sonya, Gary, Jake, the band have helped me find my voice. Proper food and meditation have nurtured me. I know now that healing can happen under the light of Mildred's purple cosmic ray. Healing can happen in dreams and in poems, on a level that is not material. I want to explore my dreams and what they mean, how they might help me on my path.

Maybe there is more than one way to change my life, more than one way to change the culture, racism, sexism. Maybe, if I work enough, I could find words to inspire people and the world to change, the way that I continue to be changed by books and words. Maybe that is where I will learn to love, to start with vulnerability on the page and grow to find it in the rest of my life.

Maybe, instead of fighting, instead of the violence that has been the strategy of last resort, maybe, just maybe, we can evolve to love!

For Berkeley, my true home.

Acknowledgments

Thank you to Justin Loeber, Principal of MOUTH Digital and PR for helping me realize that *Outside Voices* is a story worth telling, and for his stalwart support and friendship.

To my agent Nancy Rosenfeld of AAA Books Unlimited and Adriana Senior, my Editor at Post Hill Press, thank you.

My early readers, Anne Fishman and Geri Spieler, provided invaluable feedback and insights, while my friend and colleague Elizabeth Block turned out to be the surprise conduit reconnecting me with the Berkeley Women's Music Collective. Much gratitude to Nancy Vogl for taking the time to meet with me in Santa Rosa to discuss our shared history and memories. Our meetings catapulted us back to our youth and happy times! And a shoutout to all the members of the Berkeley Women's Music Collective who taught me how to walk the walk of the artist: Nancy Henderson, Susanne Shanbaum, Jake Lampert, and Debbie Lempke.

My brilliant, funny, and very *hamishe* coach and mentor, Judy Behr, has kept me on track with my writing for over twenty years.

Although writers work alone, we do not function in a vacuum—these colleagues and writing teachers have inspired and motivated me: Sandy Boucher, Tom Parker, Renate Stendhal, Jackie Berger, Deborah Grossman, Connie Post. My beloved colleagues over two

247

decades in the Women's National Book Association, particularly Brenda Knight and Elise Marie Collins have kept me in good humor and joined me in engaging in the larger literary world as have Mary Mackey, Lucy Lang Day, and Sheryl Bize-Boutte. My colleagues in Wom-ba: Katie Hafner, Barbara Quick, Lynn Kaufman, Katia Noyes, Ellen Sussman, Yang Huang, Regina Marler, Susan Wels, and over one hundred wonderful and amazing writers have provided a wonderful support network and sisterly community. Thank you to poet and writer Donna Hanelin, who helped reinvigorate my career by inviting writers to a retreat in Oaxaca, Mexico, where, in the peace of my *casita* (and with the support of the staff who did everything so that I had to do nothing but write), the first chapters of this book were written.

My friends and boosters have not only been confidantes who have walked this path with me but have made the whole enterprise worthwhile: Kelly Sullivan Walden and Dana Walden, Susan Stanger, Bea and Jerry Lott, Debbie Kinney and Julie Dorf, Plumeria Hertz, Jeff Gottesman, Kim McMillon, Nanci Cooper, Emily Klion and George Brooks, Nancy Brown and Lisa Harbus.

And a huge shout out of gratitude to the mothers of our movement: Gloria Steinem, Bella Abzug, bell hooks, Betty Friedan, Susan Sontag, Adrienne Rich—the women who were the disrupters, the loud ones—the fearless ones who shouted and fought for women's rightful place, for power over our destinies and for fighting for women to have a chance to experience success and power.